BEYOND THE GAME

Coaching for Peak Performance in Business, Sports, and Life

A gift to you from Satoshi Ochi
Sometimes the smallest step in the right direction becomes the biggest step of your life.

Rusty Komori

BEYOND THE GAME

Coaching for Peak
Performance in Business,
Sports, and Life

◆

RUSTY KOMORI

LEGACY ISLE
PUBLISHING

ISBN 978-1-948011-30-3

Library of Congress Control Number: 2019920778

Front cover photo
MaxiSports/Dreamstime

Back cover photo
Darryl Watanabe

Design and production
Angela Wu-Ki

Legacy Isle Publishing
1000 Bishop St., Ste. 806
Honolulu, HI 96813
Toll-free 1-866-900-BOOK
info@legacyislepublishing.net
www.legacyislepublishing.net

Printed in Korea

CONTENTS

FOREWORD

I believe we can all agree that leading and coaching any team effectively in business or sports is definitely challenging. Creating a positive environment in which everyone is contributing and working together towards a common goal is easier said than done.

As head coach for the Punahou boys varsity tennis team from 1994 to 2015, Rusty Komori led his teams to win an unprecedented 22 consecutive state championships. In his previous book, *Beyond the Lines*, he explained his leadership culture through the 4 Ps and the eight keys of achieving and sustaining success, which allowed his teams to accomplish these extraordinary results. He has proven experience, and his mentoring serves as a powerful resource for teams to use in helping them reach their goals.

Rusty believes that his first priority was developing champion athletes of character first, and great tennis players second. As an educator and president of Saint Louis School, I completely agree. Developing our students' character—having the right principles, values, and disciplines—is my top priority as well. I appreciate that Rusty has set such high standards for himself and his teams, focusing on moral character to help them in sports and, more importantly, in life.

Whether you're a CEO or a business team member, a coach or an athlete, a parent or a student, how do you inspire yourself and others to constantly strive for a culture of excellence? In this sequel volume, *Beyond the Game*, Rusty goes further and beyond, highlighting the importance of striving for a superior culture of excellence with what he calls "superior disciplined details." His 3 Cs of Leadership are eminently relatable and will enhance every team's culture in guiding them towards greatness. In sharing his 6 Keys of

Peak Performance, Rusty provides insights and clarity into how he was able to help every player on every team strive for maximum potential. His examples and real-life stories resonate and connect, offering valuable lessons and important takeaways.

Rusty identifies the major characteristics of some of the world's most successful leaders and weaves those attributes into the lessons he learned as Hawai'i's most successful high school coach. *Beyond the Game* is a tremendous resource for everyone in business, sports, and life. I highly recommend this book for all leaders, coaches, and students who want to improve themselves and their teams to achieve their goals and strive for the highest levels of excellence.

Dr. Glenn Medeiros
Singer and producer
President, Saint Louis School

CHAPTER 1

Make an Impact

"Everybody is standing, but you must stand out."
—Israelmore Ayivor

You are a coach if you're in a position of influence. The question is how good a coach are you? The best CEOs in business and the best head coaches in sports are always finding ways to better themselves and their teams. They're always searching for ways to be more effective and efficient. Complacency is never an issue with them. They're on a constant quest to go "beyond the lines" (you might recognize that as the title of my first book) in building deeper trust, respect, and purpose with their teams. Results, productivity, and winning become a by-product of going beyond the lines, and that's how you achieve and sustain success with your team. Ultimately, every coach should be striving to further develop and enhance the character, self-discipline, and habits of every team member, giving them the tools to help others in turn.

Before you can coach people effectively, you need to coach yourself first. How can you build and train championship qualities in others if you yourself don't possess those qualities? Your talk would be meaningless to your team and you'd be perceived as hypocritical and ineffective. Walking the walk is essential before talking the talk. Team members need to see you as someone with championship qualities and habits, in order for you to help instill those same qualities and habits in them. This will make you real and relevant to them, which sets up the foundation for you to build a championship culture for peak performance with your team.

What is Your Impact?

Are you making a difference in society? Are you having a positive impact on others every day? If you didn't show up at work today, would people miss you? If you're on a football team and you're not at the game with your team, would their odds of winning the game be a little lower because of your absence? You never truly know what your impact is on others until situations like these occur. If you believe in God, I'm sure He didn't create you just for you to be average. I'm sure He didn't create you to just take up space in this world. God wants you to make a positive impact, and the way you make a positive impact in this world is by making a positive impact on others.

If the coach leads with fairness and is someone the team members respect, every person on the team will have a deeper connection and commitment to the team, because two things are happening: They're doing something they're good at and they feel appreciated. Moreover, if they feel like they're making an impact by improving their lives and making other people's lives better, then they know they're doing something extremely meaningful. Think about it. This is something I strive for with my teams every single day. I let each individual know what their strengths are so that they know what they're good at and how they can help our team. I also let them know that it's imperative to keep building their strengths. Their mindset should never be complacent; I want them always thinking about ways to make their strengths even more effective. The strengths you have as a team allow you to be in a position to achieve success, which is why it's important to keep building these strengths.

Making someone feel appreciated is paramount. Everyone wants to feel like they matter. It's good to get a pat on the back. People need to feel that they're making a difference.

A positive difference! I would do this by genuinely complimenting my players and telling them that I notice their effort and dedication, not only in improving themselves, but also in encouraging and helping their teammates. You, as the leader, might notice these things, but you also need to articulate them. That's the key.

As head coach of the Punahou School boys varsity tennis team for 22 years, I only missed one match. It was in April 2014 against Mid-Pacific Institute. The reason was my induction into Creighton University's Hall of Fame in Omaha, Nebraska. I didn't want to miss even a single match because my team was my priority as head coach. Honors and awards are nice but not a priority for me. I shared the news about the induction with my players and it was they who convinced me to go. They reminded me that this was a special honor, that I needed to be at the induction, and that they would "take care of business" on the tennis court. They did and we defeated Mid-Pacific 4–1. I was away from my team for three days and when I returned to practice, they all told me how much they'd missed me. I knew I was making an impact. A positive impact!

Parents are Coaches

If you're a parent, you're a coach. You are coaching your sons and daughters in life. It's parents who first shape the fundamental character foundations of their children. For me, as a tennis coach, I can enhance kids' lives by further developing their character and building championship habits in them. I can create a culture of excellence and guide them in practices and matches. I can also coach the parents to reinforce what we are striving towards. We are all on the same team with the same ultimate goals—to give their sons or daughters a priceless, positive experience on the team and help them in developing their full potential as people.

Through the years, I have encountered and worked with literally thousands of parents—all types of parents. Almost all of them have the right goals to provide for their kids and hope that they will find their passion and develop their full potential in life. But why do some kids behave inappropriately? Why do some kids fall far short in reaching their full potential? Why do some kids go off on the wrong tangents and get into trouble or do bad things to others?

The answer is a variety of reasons. Yes, there are good and bad people in this world and no doubt there always will be. A newborn baby is innocent and ready to be coached and trained by Mom and Dad. A newborn isn't born with prejudice or bad character. It's the parents' responsibility to coach their kids properly early on in life. But despite the best intentions, there are still bad parents in the world. If your kids go astray, go off on wrong tangents, and do bad things to others, don't blame them. Blame yourself.

Remember that no matter who you are or how good you think you are, you can always be replaced. A CEO of a failing business can be fired in hopes that a new leader will save the company and make it profitable. A sports team with multiple losing seasons will often fire the head coach in hopes that the new coach will turn things around by winning championships. Children, however, cannot fire their parents. Still, everyone can be accountable for his or her own actions.

As a coach, I take full responsibility for all of my players' actions on the team, good and bad. As a parent, you need to do the same. That goes for the CEO of a company too. Taking accountability for yourself and your team actually teaches others to take accountability for themselves. It's walking the walk. People see what you do and how you do it. Sometimes the most impactful coaching comes through your own actions. Think about a little boy or girl watching his or her parents treating others with kindness and respect. What message do you think that boy or girl learns from watching that action? Now think about that little boy or girl watching their parents being disrespectful and mean to others. What do you think they learn from that action? Yes, kids do tend to emulate their parents, believing that their parents' actions are acceptable and appropriate. That's the power the leader has and why it's crucial to be aware of every action you take, because of the message it sends to others. I always remind parents not to protect their children from adversity, but rather to teach them how to face it. Life is challenging and they will definitely experience many adversities in their own lives. It's inevitable.

While coaching more than a thousand students over the past three decades, I also coached many of their parents to help me reinforce what I was instilling in their sons and daughters. For example, parents should reward the behavior and attitude, not the result. I've found that when you reward and value good sportsmanship, respect for your opponent, effort, resiliency, positivity, courage, fight, and toughness, this keeps everyone on the right track to do the things that are most important—to be genuinely good people. Incidentally, encouraging these great behaviors directly affects performance, which leads to better results and winning. I was always most proud when players of mine would win sportsmanship trophies (and I would make a big deal about it) because it was an acknowledgment that others recognized their amazing character.

It's also clear to me that parents shouldn't give their kids everything they want. They need to teach them the value of hard work and to appreciate things more. If everything is given to them, they will take things for granted and not truly appreciate working hard for something they really want. Having kids do household chores such as washing dishes, taking out the garbage, and doing laundry are simple yet important things that every child should be doing in every family. I did these things and also mowed lawns and washed cars for my neighbors as a teenager to earn money. As a parent, saying the word "no" is often valuable in teaching and guiding kids. Why do some kids become spoiled and feel entitled? It's because the parents give them everything they want without having to work for it. The best kids are the ones who work hard for something they want and appreciate the effort and time they put into it.

During my freshman through junior years in high school, I needed to ride our City & County's express bus to and from school, which took around an hour and a half each way. Once I got my driver's license, I must have asked my parents a hundred times to please let me drive to school instead of having to catch the bus. Their response consistently was, "No, you need to take the bus." At the start of my senior year, my parents finally allowed me to borrow my grandfather's old Dodge. It was brown and looked like an old man's car, which it was. But in my mind, I appreciated having a car and not having to ride the bus anymore, sleeping in a little bit longer, and being able to save time on my commute. The car's air-conditioning was broken, and I perspired a lot driving home from school in the Hawaiian afternoon sun. Because of this, I also appreciated cars with air-conditioning. I told myself that someday when I could afford to buy my own car, it would be one with a functioning air-conditioning unit. Because of this experience, today I definitely appreciate having the freedom to drive where I want, when I want—and with air-conditioning!

Making Good People Great

Since retiring as head coach from Punahou in 2015, I have been doing what I set out to do since I left—helping people in business, sports, and life in general. I like helping good people and making them great. I like coaching great people and making them extraordinary. And I want to inspire you to do the same. But how is it done?

After reading my first book, *Beyond the Lines: Creating a Leadership Culture to Achieve Extraordinary Results*, many CEOs invited me to be a guest speaker for their companies, because they obviously care about making their teams better. They also purchased books for all of their team members, which is absolutely fantastic as it demonstrates that the CEO cares about them and their self-improvement. The CEO wants to help the organization in striving to improve each individual, which makes the entire team better collectively. They're on the right track, seeking more clarity and better alignment in hopes of achieving greater success for their organization and sustaining that success.

There's a famous exchange between a CFO and a CEO where the CFO asks, "What happens if we invest in developing our people and then they leave us?" The CEO responds, "What if we don't and they stay?" Some relationships we have with people will last forever and some have expiration dates. The best leaders and coaches will invest time and money in their people. You can't control whether a team member will stay on your team or leave. Obviously, if you had a choice, you would want them to stay. But you always need to do things that are in the best interest of your people in order to help them. Your impact will be positive, valuable, and long-lasting, and they will always remember and be grateful for the help that you gave them.

Another way of helping to improve your people and your organization is to hire a leadership/character coach. Since my book became available, I have met with countless CEOs and business owners, head coaches of sports teams, and parents—all of whom have great principles, values, and discipline, but don't know how best to use them to help their team effectively. They obviously are amazing people who care about bettering themselves and the people around them—but there's a gigantic difference between being a great person and a great leader. Always remember: If you think it's too expensive to hire an expert, just wait and see what happens if you enlist the services of an amateur, or if you do nothing. You get what you pay for, and there's no substitute for quality and priceless guidance. The greatest leaders care deeply about their people and will always find ways to help them consistently improve.

When I meet with business leaders, I ask them what they feel are the top three things their company does that makes their organization successful. Once they share their insights with me, I ask them to rate those three areas on a scale of one to ten. I'm usually amazed that their ratings are sometimes only average to above average, often in the five to seven range—and yet these are the three things their company is known for! Every elite organization and team should have at least one area that they can honestly rate themselves in the nine to ten range.

Even moderately successful teams, who may be only average in a number of areas, should be outstanding in at least one area. Once they attain a high standard of excellence in that one area, it often becomes contagious for other areas in the organization. The potential for improvement in these companies is huge. They can visualize being much more effective and efficient with other team members and with clients. They can have a much better attention to detail. They can execute at a higher level. Once I highlight it in this way, it becomes very clear to these executives that they can choose to improve their organization in specific areas that allow them noticeably higher, more quantifiable levels of success.

A good example of this is Hawaiian Airlines, which at one point was becoming known as a second-rate airline, especially for its late departures and arrivals, and ultimately filed for bankruptcy in 2003. Two years later, Mark Dunkerley was appointed Hawaiian's CEO. Dunkerley's focus was on-time performance, because in his mind there was no excuse for not being punctual in Hawai'i, with its consistently good weather year-round. Under his leadership Hawaiian Air soon became number one in the United States for on-time arrivals and a global leader for on-time performance. Achieving this rating was extremely significant, as he transformed what had been known as a second-rate airline into one that is now second to none. The company emerged from bankruptcy in 2005 and became hugely profitable, earning gross revenues of $2.64 billion during Dunkerley's 15-year tenure. I always say that everything starts with the head coach or CEO, and it's definitely true in this case. Mark Dunkerley is praised and credited for turning a failing airline into one that is achieving excellence in many categories, but it all started because they began to excel in one category first—on-time arrivals.

Speaking of successful business leaders, Sir Richard Branson is the founder of the Virgin Group, which encompasses more than 400 companies. His businesses have impacted all of us at some point in our lives. In 2000, Branson was knighted at Buckingham Palace for his entrepreneurship in land, air, sea, and space travel. "When I started Virgin from a basement in West London," Branson once told an interviewer, "there was no great plan or strategy. I didn't set out to build a business empire. For me, building a business is all about doing something to be proud of, bringing talented people together and creating something that's going to make a real difference to other people's lives."

Every team is a reflection of their leader. If there's dysfunction, low morale, and high turnover in a company, blame the CEO and the executives. They're the people responsible for their team. They're the coaches. A weak, ineffective leader will blame others when in fact it's the leaders' fault for not finding a way to lead effectively. On the other hand, if a company has loyalty, high morale, and a culture of excellence, give all the credit in the world to the CEO and his or her executives. They're the leaders who know how to coach.

Risk Determines Destiny

What do you want to achieve and what do you need to do to achieve it? If you want to improve, you can't continue doing the same thing over and over again. You don't achieve greater success by being complacent and you can't sustain it either by doing the same thing. Once you achieve success or win a championship, other teams will try to emulate you. You just created a blueprint of success for others to follow. Every successful person and championship team has taken risks— calculated risks—to improve on their success.

Think about it. A basketball player who has never attempted a potentially game winning shot is definitely taking a risk. If the player misses, the team loses; if he makes it, they win. When LeBron James experienced this situation for the first time many years ago, I'll bet even he felt uncomfortable and nervous. Since then, he's been in this same situation time and time again, but now turning the uncomfortable into comfortable and nervousness into excitement. It becomes exciting to him because he thrives under pressure and looks forward to it. Obviously, he's made many game winning shots and he's also missed many. But how do you want to live your life? What do you want to accomplish? LeBron became LeBron because he has taken risks to achieve his success. He makes a positive impact, which inspires and encourages people around him to do the same.

Think about when you were in your youth on a basketball court by yourself shooting hoops, imagining there are three seconds left in the game and it's up to you to take the game winning shot. You count *three, two, one* and shoot the ball. Whether it goes through the hoop or not, it's the action of trying that matters. Obviously, we know there's a big difference in practice and in a game when it really counts. But having the imagination to do it in practice often leads you to have the courage to take a risk in a game. When you keep putting yourself in that position a second, third, and fourth time, you deal with the situation better each time, which leads to success. Can you imagine if you never tried? Then you'd have zero chance of improvement and no chance for success.

In an interview, Apple cofounder Steve Jobs talked about how taking risks affected his company when he started it with his business partner, Steve Wozniak. "There's no risk," he said. "That's why you need to do it young and that's why we started Apple. We said, you know, we have absolutely nothing to lose. I was 20 years old, and Woz was 24. We have no families, no children, no houses—Woz had an old car, I had a Volkswagen van. I mean, all we were going to lose was our cars and the shirts off our back. We had nothing to lose and we had everything to gain. And we figured even if we crash and burn and lose everything, the experience will have been worth ten times the cost. So there was no risk. I think that's a healthy way to look at it. The only thing you have in your life is time and if you invest that time in yourself—to have great experiences that are going to enrich you—then you can't possibly lose. So I always advise people, 'Don't wait.' Do something when you're young when you have nothing to lose and don't have the responsibilities to other people that you will acquire later on in your life." 🪙

CHAPTER 2

COACHING VS. TEACHING

"A coach is someone who tells you what you don't want to hear, who has you see what you don't want to see, so you can be who you have always known you could be."
—Tom Landry

I have great respect for teachers and their commitment to helping students in their classroom. We have all learned from teachers in our past and many of them have made positive, lasting impacts on us. I have stories about some great teachers I have had and I'm sure you have similar stories as well. Some teachers help students learn specific subjects like math, science, and history, while other teachers help them learn specific skills such as violin, dance, golf, swimming, and yes, tennis.

The point is this: There's a significant difference between teaching and coaching. A coach is a teacher who inspires a person or team through learning and guides them to be successful in life. While teachers usually focus on helping students with specific subjects and skills, coaches help students with the whole person, not just the parts. For me as a tennis coach, I focus on training the entire player—physical skills, mental toughness, emotional awareness, strategy, and tactics, not to mention developing character, dealing with the environment, losing with grace and winning with humility, being a team player, and other important traits.

I can visualize a world where everyone becomes a coach; teachers become coaches in their classrooms and business executives transform from managers into coaches for their team members, with the priority of helping the entire person, not just part of the person. I believe that more often than not, coaches of sports teams have much greater impact on their team members than teachers in the classroom. After all, an athlete typically spends significantly more time with his team and his coach than he does with his math teacher. A student might have a one-hour math class three days a week, but that same student might have football practice two hours a day Monday through Friday, in addition to games on Saturday. Because of time spent with the team, coaches' influence on the players and their development are extremely impactful. Ideally, this will have a positive, priceless effect.

Some teachers have a passion for teaching—they're great at doing what they do, and that's fine. An assistant manager might be fantastic doing what he does and doesn't want more responsibility—the general manager's job, for instance—and that's fine. An assistant coach might be valuable in that role and might not want to be a head coach, and that's fine too. The point is this. These people have found their passion and have no interest in promotions, advancements, or more responsibilities. Not everyone aspires to become a CEO or head coach. But every role matters in your organization, and you can always enhance and improve the role you're in.

Coach Them to Coach Themselves

As a tennis professional and coach, I obviously love tennis, but I also enjoy all sports. I love watching the different dynamics between coaches and athletes, especially when the pressure mounts in competition. For example, in football when the game gets chaotic and hectic, what do you see the coach do? He calls a timeout to settle the team down. Well, in tennis, we have no timeouts. In basketball, the coach puts a team of five players on the court, but what does the coach do if one of his athletes is playing badly? He or she subs in a different player. In tennis, we have no substitutions. If I could have had timeouts and substitutions, I would have used them thousands of times.

Because of this, preparation was paramount for us. I needed to coach my players to coach themselves. Once I put my athlete on the tennis court for competition, all I could really do was watch. At the state championship, coaching is not allowed during the match, except between sets. On many occasions, I would be in agony watching my players because I felt like I was playing the match. I could almost feel an ulcer or a swollen appendix coming on, because I'd feel the impact of every ball hit myself. I'd be squeezing internally, hoping that our shots would go in—but also hoping that my players would behave properly and play hard and smart from the first serve until match point.

One of the most important things about preparation is controlling everything that you can control. Worrying about things beyond your control is completely useless and leads to mental and physical fatigue. Coaching and training your team members to focus only on things within their control is key. In business, a team member might feel unnecessary pressure because they're not hitting their projected sales numbers. Now think about what this team member might begin to imagine. Because she isn't hitting the numbers, she might begin to think that her job is in jeopardy. You as the leader need to be aware of these thoughts, which will definitely inhibit performance. She may hit the numbers a week or two later, but you need to reassure her that you believe in her and that her job is secure.

It's up to you as the coach to train good habits and make certain that your team members are focused on the right things. It sounds easy but it's not. It takes awareness from the coach to consistently be in touch with the pulse and vibe of their team. I would constantly tell my players to "take care of business on our side of the net." Of course we'd be aware of what our opponent was doing, but our primary focus was on what we did. If we can control everything within our control, it will lead us to executing better, which leads to winning.

The 3 Cons

People often talk about the pros and cons of a situation. Well, I assure you that these "3 Cons" are positive and absolutely necessary for coaches to help enhance each team member's commitment and experience with the team. When each team member practices these 3 Cons, trust and loyalty become deeper and team excellence becomes higher. What are the 3 Cons? They're Contribute, Consistency, and Confidence. Every coach must instill these in each individual to help the players and the team achieve and sustain peak performance. Once this happens, it often becomes contagious, because each team member will have a tendency to encourage and help other team members do what their leader did for them.

Contribute. People on a team want to feel that they're making a difference. They want to feel that what they're doing is important and impactful. Think about it. If every team member is contributing to the purpose and striving to accomplish the goals of the team, it becomes meaningful to them because each person matters. Each person must contribute and do his or her part in helping the team achieve success. It's the coach's responsibility to share with each team member how important their role is in order for the team to achieve its goals.

As head coach, I would meet with each team member, asking them to tell me what they think their strengths are. I find it amazing at times how some people don't know what their strengths are. And sometimes, what they think is a strength might not actually be one. After listening to what they say, I share with them what I feel their strengths are and how they can contribute to our team's success. Once they know their strengths and how they can contribute, they feel more valued.

In a company, even the janitor plays an important role. Imagine if the workspace is dirty or messy. How would your company be perceived by your own employees and others? It's necessary to acknowledge every person who plays a role and affects your team. A CEO and other team members who take five seconds to tell the janitor how much he appreciates him keeping things extra clean and orderly will make that person feel important. The janitor will feel valued because of that simple acknowledgment and will want to keep doing the best job possible.

It's crucial that the best CEOs always make time to spend time with their frontline team members. If you're a leader, you can always take a minimum of 20 minutes daily to be visible and talk with them. This needs to be a priority. You can show empathy by asking them meaningful questions: How's your family doing? Did your mom recover well from surgery? What can I do to help you perform your job better? It allows you to stay in touch with what's happening on the front lines. It shows that you care and value them. It shows them that what they do plays a key role in the success of your company.

Let me share with you what I did with my team regarding individual contributions. When we play a duel match against another school, we have 1st and 2nd singles, and 1st, 2nd, and 3rd doubles (best of five wins). Well, oftentimes my 2nd singles player wants to play 1st singles and my 3rd doubles team wants to play 2nd doubles and 2nd doubles wants to play 1st doubles. Remember how I want every player to feel important? How do I keep everyone happy to be playing in the position they need to play in?

First of all, in the beginning of our season, we play singles challenge matches to establish a fair rank order on our team. This is important for integrity and fairness among my team and to provide an honest, correct roster for our opponents. Secondly, from this team ranking, I'll select my singles and doubles players. I like sharing with the team why I feel these players in these positions can help our team achieve our goal of winning a state championship. Because of my communication with them, they know exactly what I'm thinking and there are no misunderstandings. Thirdly, connecting players together as doubles partners can be challenging. They need to buy in to playing with and helping each other. Therefore, I'll weigh my options and look for the best fit among doubles teams as possible. I always prefer to have a power player with a control player (instead of having two power players together or two control players together).

Once we get through these situations and compete in a duel match, my 3rd doubles team might feel like they're at the bottom of the lineup, even though we have four more players on our team not in the starting lineup that day. This is when I'll share with them how hugely important 3rd doubles is to the success of our team. I'll tell them that although the spotlight is usually on 1st singles and 1st doubles, it's actually 2nd singles, 2nd doubles, and 3rd doubles that I am depending on to bring us a victory. Those three positions are critical for us to win. I'll share with them that if we win in those three positions, then we win as a team regardless of what happens in 1st singles or 1st doubles. Sometimes other teams have better players playing in those top positions and they might beat us in those individual matches, but we will win as a team because we'll win the other three. When I explain it in this way, every player understands how important every position is. They all want to win—ideally they want to win 5–0, because nobody really enjoys losing. Even the players not in the lineup that day will be cheering and supporting their teammates because everyone is valued and everyone contributes.

Think about the bigger picture and ask yourself, "How can I contribute to society? How can I make the world a better place?" We should all want to help other people and do things in a better way to ultimately leave a legacy for others to follow. When you think about it, it's really a privilege to be in this world and an even bigger privilege to be in the United States. If there's any doubt, just look at how many people from other countries want to emigrate to America.

Consistency. There are two types of consistency. The first is consistency of performance of the coach and team members, which leads to higher productivity, better results, and winning. My team members expected consistency from me and I expected the same from them. Being unpredictable with them is not good in this case because they want to see consistency with my words and actions. They want me to follow through and do the things that I said I would do. They want their leader to be reliable, honest, and trustworthy. In terms of developing my team members, I would focus on improving the fundamentals of my players, because that leads to consistency in their performance, especially when the pressure is on. When there is pressure and a player has weak fundamentals, it is extremely visible. The same is true in business and in life.

The second is consistency in following up with your team members. A coach might schedule a meeting with a team member to focus on personal development to help that person make their strengths stronger and strive to improve on a weakness. This only helps if there are follow-up meetings to track improvement. Consistency is key! How many times have you had a meeting with someone and there is no follow-up? Things might improve briefly before what little progress was made begins to quickly fade away.

You might be thinking that this might consume a lot of time. It doesn't. Oftentimes, I'll do a quick follow-up with my player that takes less than one minute, but the impact is huge. It doesn't have to be a scheduled half-hour meeting or anything of that sort. Sometimes casual is better and more comfortable. For example, as I'm walking by I would say, "Hey, Matt, how's that one thing coming along that we talked about." Matt knows that because I'm following up with him, it must be important to me, which shows that it should be a priority for him. It also shows that I care about him and his development.

How many times have you heard someone say they are going to do something and it doesn't get done? This drives me nuts! How do you think your team will respond to you? When you say you're going to do something, do it! Your words should mean something. The best coaches do what they say— always. This is part of consistency. As a coach, you need to be the example to your team. You are their role model. Words and actions matter. Little things matter. Little things lead to little victories. And, little victories lead to big victories.

Having consistency with your team members is absolutely necessary in moving your team in the right direction to accomplish the team's goals. The greatest leaders always have the best interests of their team members at heart, and consistently know what they want and need. You are building other great leaders who may or may not be with you forever, and that's OK. You care about them and their improvement and they know it.

Confidence. Once your team members know how they're contributing and you have consistency to keep moving everyone in the right direction, building their confidence leads to empowerment. People become confident when they know they're good at something and they know they are supported. Think about you and what gives you confidence. Now think about doubt. Letting doubt enter your mind is a confidence killer. That's why your mindset is so important. You need to always focus on what you want to achieve and avoid unnecessary noise and distractions. Tunnel vision is good. Believe in yourself!

When Punahou School athletic director Chris McLachlin and tennis director Bernard Gusman asked me to be head coach of our boys varsity tennis team, I felt confident that they believed in me and that they knew I could do the job and do it well. They didn't micromanage me, and I felt 100 percent supported with all of my decision-making. They are both great leaders who trusted me and I felt empowered and did not want to disappoint them. I wanted to make them and Punahou School proud. I wanted to be the best version of me that I could possibly be, and they gave me confidence through their words and actions.

This is why it's important for CEOs to give responsibility to their executives and for the executives to give responsibility to the directors, the managers, and the people on the front line. By doing this, you are showing that you have confidence in others to get the job done. They, in turn, should be the best they can be to not let their leader down. If and when a mistake happens, it's an opportunity for learning, and the leader must always be available for advice and support. However, with both championship teams and elite organizations, it's unacceptable if the same mistake is made twice. Team members should have the freedom to innovate and try new things to make the team better, and not be afraid to make a mistake. They just need to learn from it so it doesn't happen again.

The word "encouragement" can be defined as the act of instilling courage in another. When you give encouragement to someone, you are showing that you believe they can do it because you have faith in them and they should believe in themselves. This simple act is extremely powerful and leads to building confidence in whatever they want to achieve, no matter how great the odds might be. If you think you can do it, you have a chance. If you think you can't, you have no chance. Giving thoughtful and genuine encouragement to each other will give your team opportunities to achieve greatness.

Ashley Ishimura

Years ago, I began coaching a seven-year-old girl named Ashley Ishimura in private tennis lessons. She had a passion for tennis, worked extremely hard, and listened well. Yes, three great ingredients to have in any student, for sure. But Ashley was not a gifted athlete, as many others are. I would consider her a blue-collar player with above average talent for tennis. My main goal was to keep things fun for her. Nobody wants to do something that's not fun. I knew that if she continued to have fun with tennis, she would keep improving. My second goal was to work on developing her fundamentals and building an all-court game.

I trained Ashley one to two times a week and after a few years, she was ready and eager to enter tournaments. The first tournament I watched her compete in was at the Hale Koa Hotel in Waikīkī, playing in the age ten and under division. Although she was physically prepared, it was going to be a test to see where she was mentally and emotionally. She

Coach Rusty with Ashley Ishimura

was excited for her first match, and I knew it was going to
be a definite learning experience. She competed well but her
opponent had more tournament experience and made some
questionable line calls on some key points, which affected
Ashley. After losing the match, Ashley shook hands with her
opponent, walked off the court, came directly to her parents
and me, and began to cry. I feel that crying is actually a good
thing because it shows me that she cares. After consoling her,
I asked her if she wanted to play another tournament in a few
weeks and she said, "Yes!" I knew right then that this was going
to be a long-lasting and memorable journey together.

Through the years—including many more tears after
some tough defeats in matches—Ashley was learning about
life through tennis. She learned the value of hard work, perseverance, and sacrifice. She learned to be resilient, to never
give up, and the importance of a positive attitude. She learned

to win with humility and lose with grace. All of this because I was coaching all of her, not just teaching a part of her. She knew that I was honest and could trust me. And she knew that I always had her best interests in mind. The touching thing to me was she looked at me as more than a coach—and often conveyed that I was like a second father to her. Talk about making an impact!

If I fast-forward a few years, Ashley attended Punahou School, made the Punahou School girls varsity tennis team as a freshman, and was number one on the varsity team all four years. After graduating from high school in 2015, Ashley earned a partial tennis scholarship to Creighton University in Omaha, Nebraska (Yes, that's where I went to college on a partial tennis scholarship as well). My former college roommate and current head coach at Creighton, Tom Lilly, recruited her. I told him that as good as Ashley was in tennis, she was an even better person, with outstanding character. She was an amazing team player who was selfless and had a team first mentality. Although she received full scholarship offers from other universities, she felt a great connection with Creighton, especially after meeting with Coach Tom and his wife, Jean, on a college visit. Since arriving at Creighton as a freshman, Ashley mirrored her experience in high school and was number one on the tennis team all four years. She recently graduated with a business degree in finance and, needless to say, I'm so very proud of her and the person I helped her become through coaching her in tennis and in life. 🎾

THE 3 CS OF LEADERSHIP

◆

"The greatest leader is not necessarily the one who does the greatest things. He is the one that gets the people to do the greatest things."

—Ronald Reagan

CHAPTER 3

CHOICES

"And in life, it is all about choices we make.
And how the direction of our lives comes down
to the choices we choose."
—Catherine Pulsifer

Not long ago I had dinner with my friend Jennifer, who complained about a client who was extremely rude and mean to her on a phone call. She shared with me that while she continued to be professional and positive, internally she was feeling upset and disrespected. She also shared with me that her phone call with that client lasted for only four minutes but ruined the rest of her day. My response to her was, "Why would you let a bad four minutes affect the rest of your day?" There was another 23 hours and 56 minutes that she allowed those four minutes to affect. And, she was probably affecting other clients, coworkers, and family members because of how those four minutes bothered her. Obviously, she still wasn't over it because she was now venting to me, and this incident had happened weeks before.

Once I asked her that question, everything started to make sense. She reflected on how that one incident was affecting various parts of her life. She could clearly see how she was revisiting that incident daily. I told her she had a choice to make. She needed to choose to let it go and move on, and that's exactly what she did. I told her that the lesson here is to never let a bad four minutes ruin your day. We all have had and will continue to have similar unfortunate interactions with people that might make us feel how Jennifer felt. The great thing is that we have a choice in how we respond.

Take Calculated Risks

I've spoken with countless people who feel stuck in their lives, whether it's a job in which they dislike their manager or a sports team with a bad coach. Sometimes we become so consumed in our daily routines that we forget that we have the power of choice. We can make a change. We don't have to be stuck in that situation every day for the rest of our lives. And yes, it's often scary and frightening to make a change and do something different to possibly make your life better. Think of the alternative if you do nothing. You will continue to add misery to your life, and probably the lives of others, because of that unfair manager or coach.

Everything we do, every choice and decision we make, involves some level of risk. But remember, risk promotes growth and risk determines destiny. You can choose complacency or you can choose to try something different. What do you think successful people do? What do you think champions do? They're never complacent and always have courage to make proper choices to align with the goals they want to achieve. When you make these better and new choices, you give yourself an opportunity for new experiences and new feelings. These new experiences and feelings lead to bigger and better things you wouldn't have discovered had you chose the status quo.

There are three main categories of choices you can make that will keep you on the right path in life: mindset, health, and personal growth. We only get one mind and one body when we enter this world. It's not like trading in an old car for a new car. We can't trade in an old body for a new one. We need to take care of the body and mind we're given. Whenever you can make these daily choices in improving your mindset, health, and personal growth, you will continue to head in the right direction in living a better life.

Let me identify some examples of choices you can make for yourself right now. You can choose to be positive and have a favorable outlook on life. You can choose to focus on finishing something that you started. You can choose to eat healthier, which will make you feel better about yourself. You can choose to exercise more, which will add to improving your health and fitness. You can choose to learn something new by reading a book (which you're obviously doing right now) or attending a seminar, which is an opportunity for learning and personal growth. You can choose to help somebody and do something nice for that person, which adds to your personal fulfillment. Think about the alternatives to these examples if you don't choose wisely.

Once you make these choices, you need to commit and do it consistently until it becomes a habit. A winning attitude is a habit, but so is a losing one. So how do you build good habits? According to a study done years ago, when you have a thought about doing something, you only have three to five seconds to do it or your brain actually starts to talk you out of doing it. Think about how true this is. How many times have we thought about going for a run—but instead we check Instagram? Or we think about going to the gym and instead we turn on the television. Once you have a thought about doing something productive, train yourself to do it immediately. It's as simple as that.

The greatest coaches are constantly finding ways to be better and they take calculated risks to improve themselves and their team. They take nothing for granted and outdo what they have done. Trying different things to see what works and what doesn't work is a good thing. What's costly is doing nothing new and being idle. These great coaches also know that there are consequences for every choice you make. There's a cause and effect, and effects from effects. You need to look at the big picture as well as the smaller segments and then connect the dots to stay on the right path.

Look Ahead

As a coach, it's imperative to always look ahead to what you want to accomplish in life, and to train your team members to do the same. It's like driving a car. There's a reason why the front windshield is so large and the rearview mirror is small. In fact, it's often tempting to look behind you into the past because there are three rearview mirrors. But your focus always has to be on what's ahead of you. Be aware of who's around you—behind and to the side—but the focus always has to be looking through that big front windshield. That's how you accomplish goals in life. Learn from your past and train yourself and others to always choose to focus on what's ahead of you.

Speaking of cars, I recently parked my own in a mall garage, and when I returned an hour later I noticed something different just above the right rear tire. Upon closer inspection, it was clear that somebody had banged my car, leaving a sizeable dent and scratch as they were trying to park next to me. There was no note, and of course I felt sick. I don't know about you, but my car is a part of me, and I felt as though I had been dented and scratched myself.

The next day I took my car to a body shop for an estimate and found that the repair job would cost $2,500. I then learned from my insurance company that I have $1,000 deductible in such situations. The sick feeling of the day before instantly became much worse. I began to think about the value of $1,000 and all the things I could buy, instead of paying an auto repair company for something that wasn't my fault. I had a choice to make. I could focus on the past, looking in the rearview mirror, and continue to let this bother me, or I could move on and look through my big front windshield at all the opportunities ahead of me. What choice did I make? Well, because I talk the talk, I must also walk the walk.

Training yourself and your team to make a conscious choice in controlling what you think, say, and do keeps you on the path towards peak performance. This type of self-control was an important discipline and habit I consistently worked on with my team, practically on a daily basis. I would tell them, "If we can control our thoughts, mouths, and hands, we have a great chance of controlling the tennis ball."

Think about how this simple concept affects us in life. This was a big part of our success because I wanted us to think properly, speak intelligently, and only do things that would help us achieve our goal. Many teams do things to hinder their performance by shooting themselves in the foot unnecessarily. Bad choices help teams lose, so shouldn't we choose only those things that help us win? It seems logical, and it needs to become a habit of self-discipline and self-control. Having this awareness and always choosing the high road regardless of the circumstances is a valuable habit to own.

Be Resourceful

Punahou School is known as a private school with a public purpose. We welcome teachers and coaches from other schools to come and see what we do to help our students. It's not just about bettering our own students, it's about helping improve our community—which could lead to improving our country and potentially the world. While I was at Punahou, this was a common occurrence for us at our tennis facility. We were very open and willing to help other schools in the US and abroad. Outside teachers and coaches would come to observe and learn why our tennis programs were very successful and then add what they'd seen to their own programs. I always remember the quote, "Helping one person might not change the world, but it could change the world for one person." I strongly believe that helping one person can be like a drop of water splashing in the ocean, causing a ripple effect to potentially help many others.

Through the years, I've been asked by coaches from other schools to participate in tennis clinics for their teams, and I've always accepted the invitation. Many of these teams are at public schools with very limited resources. Maybe their tennis balls are old, flat, and dirty, or their tennis courts are cracked and in need of resurfacing. Perhaps their players have worn-out shoes and old tennis rackets and can't afford private or group tennis lessons. And yet, it's not about having the nicest courts or fanciest uniforms or newest equipment. It's about how well you can play the game. Everyone has the same rules to abide by and the same-sized tennis court with a net in between. When I share this with these teams, it makes complete sense to them. I tell them that it really comes down to your desire for greatness. If you really want to be good or even great at something, you can. Nobody can deny you the opportunity to be great or achieve a number one ranking. It all depends on you and how bad you want it.

I would also share with these teams that no matter how little you have or how bad things appear, there's always others who have less and worse situations than you. I've seen videos of little kids learning and practicing tennis in the Philippines on tennis courts with surfaces of dirt. Many of these kids are playing tennis in flip-flops because they can't afford shoes and are using old donated tennis rackets. And yet, they have passion and a strong desire for excellence. These kids are having fun learning and improving in their sport. They have limited resources and their coach is helping them to be very resourceful and to keep the correct perspective. When I'm watching these videos on YouTube, seeing their incredible progress in developing their fundamentals, I am extremely impressed with their perseverance and commitment in wanting to be better than they were yesterday. The reason I love tennis is that it all depends on you and your passion to achieve greatness on the court and in life. The great Andre Agassi said, "It's no accident that tennis uses the language of life: advantage, service, fault, break, love…the basic elements of everyday existence, because every match is life in miniature."

Coach Dean Shimada

Coach Dean Shimada is the counselor for Waianae High School and also the head coach for their boys and girls varsity tennis teams. He's been a friend of mine for many years and is a man of outstanding character. Last year, he asked me to be a guest speaker during one of his team practices and I gladly agreed. When I arrived at his practice, it was clear to me that all of his players were excited to be there with him and eager to get onto the courts to work on improving their tennis game.

Although Waianae High School does not have its own tennis courts on campus and needs to reserve public tennis courts for its practices, it's obvious to me that the boys and girls feel privileged to be there and greatly respect their coach. They also have limited resources but, luckily, Dean is very resourceful. He truly cares about the well-being of each team member and wants to help them make better choices not only in school and on the court, but also in life. He has their best interests at heart and empathy for them, and they know it.

As I was speaking and interacting with Dean and his team, it was clear to me that he had created a positive, safe learning environment for them. He has established a culture of excellence for his players in learning life lessons through tennis. Although tennis is an individual sport, he has created a special team where everyone plays a role and contributes to the success of the team. Success might not really be about winning (and trust me, they all obviously want to win) as it is about helping and encouraging each other to have fun and enjoy their experience together.

At the conclusion of their season, Dean invited me to the team party at Dave & Buster's and bought a copy of my first book for every boy and girl at his own expense. They were all so appreciative of this coach who many of them look up to as a second father. It's reciprocal because I can see that he cares for them as if they are his own sons and daughters. The highlight of the evening was when Dean asked his seniors to speak into a microphone, one by one. The significant thing I witnessed was not one of those seniors talked about tennis. They talked about how they felt they were part of a special family and looked forward to being with their brothers and sisters at tennis practice. They told next year's returning players that being on the team was the best choice they'd ever made in their lives, and they advised them to appreciate every day they had together. They thanked Dean's wife, Jo, and son, Alec, for allowing Dean to be their coach, acknowledging that it's time away from his family, and they thanked Dean for his commitment, time, and sacrifice to help them make better choices and improve their lives. Many of the seniors began to cry as they spoke, which caused many of us in the audience to cry as well. It was powerful. It was impactful. I was so proud of Dean and for the opportunity to witness and be a part of this priceless experience. The Waianae High School varsity tennis team might not have won the state championship, but they are definitely champions in life. 🎾

CHAPTER 4

◆

COMMUNICATION

"Words are free. It's how you use them that will cost you."
—Joshua Miller

D
o you ever notice when someone speaks, how meaningful or meaningless their communication can be? Think about someone who speaks briefly, and you listen intently to every single word. Now think about someone who speaks for 30 minutes, yet you can't remember a thing they said. Words are powerful. Silence is also powerful. What you say and how you say it makes a world of difference.

When I'm coaching my doubles teams in tennis, I want them to communicate effectively with each other. I want everything they say to each other in competition to be meaningful. For example, if Austin is serving and double-faults, Jacob might say, "Good try, Austin." Do you think this is a good response from Jacob as a doubles partner? Maybe, but it seems like a generic response to me—one that, repeated often enough, could soon become meaningless. What if, instead, Jacob says, "It's OK, Austin—on this next serve hit your slice and aim for the middle of the service box." Now this is quality communication. It's always better to focus on what to do (what you want to achieve) versus just saying "good try" and hoping things will improve.

Now the worst response from Jacob is no response. If Austin double-faults and Jacob says nothing, Austin might begin to feel bad, like he's letting Jacob down. In reality,

Austin serving a double fault might not bother Jacob at all, but Jacob's silence might lead Austin to believe that he is making Jacob mad or irritated, which might ultimately lead to Austin playing worse. And this is all because of the power of communication, or lack thereof.

As the coach, I constantly strive to say only meaningful, important things to my team members. I choose my words carefully and I find that they listen better—because they know if I say something it must be important and will result in a positive impact. Of course they know I have empathy for them, because I often asked them about how they were doing in school, about their personal goals, if everything was good in their lives, and how I could help them in those areas. Because of my open communication with them, they knew that I cared for them as much more than just tennis players. I wanted them to succeed in life, which coincidentally, helps them succeed on the tennis court.

The 4 Misses

I've seen that most problems in life happen because of what I refer to as the "4 Misses"—Miscommunication, Misunderstanding, Misperception, and Misinformation. Think about your own life and how many times you've encountered problems and dysfunction because of these 4 Misses. Think about the many times you've seen this happen with people around you. Consequently, I became proactive with my team. I shared this with them, knowing that we would definitely encounter situations that could take us on different tangents, instead of keeping us on track to achieve our goals. I could even predict the future, telling my team, "When Dan gets mad at Jimmy this season, it could easily be because of one of the 4 Misses. Maybe Dan misperceives Jimmy's intent because he didn't have all the information or all the facts."

Oftentimes when situations would arise among members of my team, it was one the other players who would recognize it and say, "They're getting mad at each other, and it's totally what Coach Rusty said about the 4 Misses." Because I was proactive in communicating to them that things can and will happen, this alone often saved us from going off on wrong tangents and dealing with unnecessary situations (and wasting valuable time), and instead kept us on the yellow brick road towards getting closer to achieving our goals.

In regards to the power of nonverbal communication, I once saw something fascinating when an elderly blind man sat down beside a busy walkway near a shopping mall. He had three things with him: a pen, cardboard sign, and coffee mug.

The message on his cardboard sign read, I'M BLIND—PLEASE HELP. I'd estimate that for every 20 people that walked by, one would stop and give him coins or maybe a dollar bill. After 30 minutes, one passerby stopped in front of the man, picked up his sign and pen, and wrote a different message on the other side. While he was writing, the blind man reached out to touch and feel this person's shoes. Though they hadn't spoken a word to one another, he now realized the passerby was a woman, who then put the sign down with its new message and continued on her way.

Now, for every 20 people that walked by, I'd estimate that 19 of them stopped and gave the man coins and dollar bills. This continued until his coffee mug began to overflow. After an hour, someone stopped and stood in front of the man, who reached out and found that it was the same woman. "Ma'am, thank you so very much," he said with excitement and gratitude. "May I ask, what is the message that you wrote?" She replied, "It's a beautiful day, and I can't see it."

We need to make certain that our message is really resonating with whomever we're communicating with. Is there a better way to communicate and reach your team members? Are you communicating correctly to inspire them to do what needs to be done? Is there a more effective way for our team members to communicate with our clients? Whether we are speaking verbally or nonverbally, communication is truly an art and we constantly need to be aware of what we say and how we say it.

Speaking of communication, I would share some wisdom with my team that they should never make fun of someone who speaks broken English—because it just means that they're proficient in another language. And here's more wisdom for you by the educator Walter Barbe, who said, "If you've told a child a thousand times, and the child still has not learned, then it is not the child who is the slow learner." All of us can definitely use words of wisdom, and we need to remember that most problems happen because of the 4 Misses. It will help you and your team stay on the right track on your quest to achieve and sustain peak performance.

Find a Connection

Effective communication is about connecting with people. People like when you understand their situation. They become more open to share their concerns and feelings with you because you can relate to them. Oftentimes, it's the leader who should first share a story of an experience that happened to them or about someone they know to allow the possibility of the other sharing something next. This sets the stage for a good back and forth interaction where you can get into the deeper issues of concern.

I remember being in a London café on a trip to Wimbledon many years ago, when the woman behind me tapped me on the shoulder and asked if I was from the States. When I said, "I am," she became excited and said, "Me too!" A few years ago, I was at a winery in Napa Valley when another customer asked me if I was from Hawai'i. I said yes and his face lit up and he said that he was from the Islands too. And when I was on a snowboarding trip in Whistler, Canada, a hotel employee asked me if I played tennis. When I responded yes, he said that he was a tennis instructor at a nearby club and we talked for a good 15 minutes about tennis.

The point is this: People like having things in common with other people. It makes them feel connected. It's the same idea when you communicate with someone. You are trying to find things in common. Maybe you both are single parents, or maybe your parents are divorced and that's what you have in common. Maybe you both are small business owners or have been in leadership positions and that's what you have in common. Maybe you both played sports or worked in finance and that's what you have in common. Finding a connection, any connection with the other, starts the formation of a common thread, which leads to the building of a strong bond.

Social media is a huge part of how we communicate and connect with people in society nowadays. Let's think about why people post on social media. The best and clearest explanation I found is by Honolulu life coach Alice Inoue. She says, "Much of what you see posted on social media is a carefully curated stream that shows a one-sided reality of what we want others to see and think about us. Whether you are aware of it or not, we post for either narcissistic or altruistic reasons. If we are feeling narcissistic, we post things that show how 'good' we are in some way—that we look good, are having a good time, are being a good parent or spouse, or that show we are in love. We hope posts like this will garner positive feedback, as we all love praise and we all want to highlight our success. If we are in an altruistic mood, we post things to help others—words of encouragement or an inspiring story, video, or photo. We hope these posts will assist others in their life journeys and that people will be appreciative, because giving and serving others makes us feel good, as well. When you are posting about the good aspects of yourself or your life, you are showing that you have value. When you are posting something to help others, you are showing others that they have value. Social media is both a projection and a reflection. The more conscious you are in what you project, the better your reflection. It's about the yin and the yang, the push and pull, the polarity of life."

Change vs. Improve

If something is not working, change is necessary. But, I often hear some leaders misuse the word "change," which could lead to confusion among members of their team. When people hear "change," they usually think that something will be different. They think that whatever they have been working on might be a waste of time because the leader now wants change. The leader should instead use the word "improve," because that's exactly what they're trying to do—unless, of course, they really want to do something completely different that warrants the proper use of the word "change." The effect is this might actually be a miscommunication by the leader, which usually leads to misperceptions and misunderstandings by team members and often causes them to not buy in and possibly reject this idea of change.

When I'm helping a tennis player with their tennis game, how I communicate is vital. For example, if I say, "Stacy, we need to change your serve." What do you think she's thinking? She's probably thinking that we are going to make her serve different and she might feel that maybe time was wasted practicing things that I had her previously working on. She might even refuse to try something new because she feels good with her current serve.

Let's try this approach. I'll say, "Stacy, we need to improve your serve." How do you think she will respond? Will she be open to hearing more about how we can improve her serve? Of course! Change scares people but everyone wants to improve. I'll often use the word "adjust" when making an improvement. For example, I'll say, "Stacy, if we adjust your grip 1/16 of an inch towards the left, it will give you more spin and power, which will allow you the opportunity to reach your full serving potential." People perceive words in different ways. Instead of using the word "adjust," what if I used the word "change?" Stacy would most likely feel uneasy about "changing" her grip for her serve. Other words that I have used similar to "adjust" are "modify," "enhance," "fine-tune," "alter," and "transform."

So keep in mind what you are trying to accomplish. Are you really trying to *change* something or are you striving to *improve* something?

A change in management is something that every team usually experiences at some point in time. If a business has a new general manager or a sports team has a new head coach, it often leads to team members feeling a bit uneasy because of the unknown. They don't know this new leader. Because of uncertainty, team members know that this change will lead to one of three situations for them: the team could get worse, stay the same, or it could improve. As their new leader, you need to know what they're probably thinking and feeling in order to communicate to them that this is a fantastic opportunity for improvement. In order to get them to buy in to your philosophy, your words and actions are extremely vital because your team will be watching everything you say and do. Connecting and sharing with them that it's an opportunity for growth, more efficiency, and deeper purpose in helping the team, both individually and collectively, will get them thinking about improvement as well. Keeping the focus on what you're striving to achieve together by involving them to contribute their creative ideas and collaborating to make the team stronger and better often gets them excited for the future with you as their new leader.

When I became head coach in 1994, I knew that I had to earn the trust and respect of every player on the team and it was obvious to me that they would be watching everything I said and did. I wanted to inspire them, get them excited about what we could accomplish together, and know that we are all a reflection of each other. I started by setting our standard of excellence and higher expectations that I had of them and that they can expect from me as well. The irony is my standard and expectations had nothing to do with winning. It was about our character, integrity and ethics, playing by the rules, and representing Punahou School with ultimate class. Speaking of rules, I shared with them that we had only two team rules: listening and lateness. I always like to keep things simple and clear. I shared, "I expect punctuality from you and you can expect the same from me. And I need you to listen to me, and I will listen to you."

This communication with my team set a tone of excitement and potential possibilities of what we could accomplish together with me as their new leader. Of course, I was dealing with high school boys, and some of them tested me regarding the consequences of not listening or being late. But this is part of discipline, and discipline is necessary for success. Needless to say, any violation of our rules resulted in consequences that greatly enhanced the violator's strength and conditioning—whether he was number one or number 12 on our team, because the rules are for everyone. And trust me, because of these consequences, they did not want to violate our rules. Again, your words and actions matter, and this helped me build trust and respect with my team and became the foundation for our success.

Travis Ing

My varsity team tryouts were very intense and I would often have 25–30 players trying out for 12 spots. When it came down to 13 players, the "sudden death" singles match would be played with the winner making the team and the loser coming only so close to making the team. One year, Travis Ing was that player who was defeated in a super close three-set match. You can imagine how devastated Travis must have felt, coming up just a little short in making the team and then having to meet with me in my office after the match.

I always tried to put myself in my player's shoes to understand what he was thinking and feeling. Needless to say, Travis was extremely disappointed and feeling down, big time. I would be too! When Travis walked into my office he was naturally going to be feeling really bad. My goal was that when he left my office, he'd be feeling good. I want people leaving a meeting with me feeling much better about themselves and their situation than when they first walk in.

Travis Ing

So let me share with you what I talked with Travis about. I said, "Travis, take a seat. Analyze the match for me. Tell me what happened."

"Coach, I know I had my opportunities and I missed some key shots on some big points. I felt really nervous and didn't feel like I played up to the level I'm capable of."

I jumped in. "Travis, you're right. But, what if this was the state singles championship and you didn't bring it today? You can't tell your opponent to come back tomorrow and let's play it again. No, you have to wait one year, maybe, to be fortunate to be in that situation again. Do you agree?"

"Yes, I know it was fair and I had my chance to win."

"Travis, every tennis player knows how it feels to lose a tough, big match. I know the feeling for sure. It's miserable! But what's done is done. It's in the past. My question for you is what are you going to do now? Are you going to quit tennis or are you going to work even harder?"

"Coach, I want to make the varsity team. It's been a huge goal of mine for many years."

"Travis, every year we have two players playing in the sudden death singles match. Do you know why?"

"Well," he said, "in the informational meeting a few weeks ago, you said it's the fairest way."

"That's right," I told him. "It's the fairest way because I don't want to make a judgement call on who makes the team. I always put myself in your shoes because if I were in your situation, I would want to control my own destiny on the tennis court. Every player that lost the sudden death match over the years immediately got on the court the next day to work on their game and practice harder than ever. They motivated themselves because they all had your same goal of wanting to make the team. And you know what? All of them came back to tryouts the following year better, stronger, and smarter, and they all made the team with no problem. It's a choice. It's your choice."

"Coach, what do I need to do to be better?" Travis asked.

"Two big things stand out to me. One is consistency. You need to have better shot tolerance and be more patient with all of your shots. You'll play a really solid point and then you'll make an unforced error on the next point. When this happens, you're no better than even. You need to win clusters of points and that's why your consistency needs to improve. Second, you need to have a stronger mindset. The brain controls the body, which will keep you in the right internal climate. The key thing here is to focus on what you want to achieve and tell yourself that you're excited, instead of getting nervous thinking about things that you hope won't happen."

"That makes sense," he said. "I'll start working on those things tomorrow."

I jumped in again, saying, "Travis, what's great about this is it's completely under your control. If you want to be great, then you can be great. If you need to be more consistent, then go practice being more consistent. If you need to improve your mindset and focus, then do that too. I'm expecting you to work on these things every day and I'm hoping you will earn your spot on our team and contribute in a big way next year."

"Thanks, Coach. I appreciate you sharing those things with me."

Travis left the office feeling hugely better than when he first walked in. The next thing I needed to do was to talk with his parents. I know they were feeling as disappointed and sad as Travis, if not more so, especially his dad, Richard. By the way, the following year Travis went through tryouts playing at a much higher level and made the team with no problem. The bottom line is I wanted everyone to feel proud and connected to Punahou boys varsity tennis, whether they were on the team or not. It only takes a little time for the coach to acknowledge players or parents, speaking sincerely with them for just a few minutes, but that exchange can have priceless effects down the road. 🎾

CHAPTER 5

CULTURE

"The strength of the team is each individual member.
The strength of each member is the team."
—Phil Jackson

When you're the coach, it's your responsibility to create the culture you want for your team. There's nothing wrong with having high standards for yourself and your team. In fact, it's definitely better to start off with a higher standard instead of a lower one. It's a good thing to be striving for limits just beyond your reach. That's what makes good people great and great people extraordinary. It's a constant striving for excellence. Think about times in your life when you thought that you couldn't accomplish something, but then you did it and had the satisfying feeling that your perseverance had paid off. That's when life becomes more meaningful, because you faced a challenge and you overcame it. Every person is capable of doing so much more than what they think they're capable of.

Because of our team's winning streak, we were definitely in the public eye. There were many people supporting us who were impressed with our culture of excellence and others wanting to see us lose, mainly because of jealousy. It's a bit like the New England Patriots—people seem to either love them or hate them just because they win a lot. But shouldn't everyone applaud them because of their high standard of excellence, consistently having a great team every year, and winning multiple Super Bowls? Sometimes it seems people just want to see a successful team lose, so they cheer against them for no good reason.

Because of our team's high visibility, I often reminded my players that we could do 99 things right, but if we did one wrong thing, everyone would only remember that one thing. That's just how it is. So I told them we could never do that one wrong thing. It's a privilege to be on top and everyone else wanting to be where we are. That's why, after we won our first state championship together, I wanted my team to focus every day on striving towards two things: a superior culture of excellence and superior disciplined details.

Superior Culture of Excellence

It's extremely important to me that everyone on my team showed empathy for each other, and I wanted to make certain that each person was valued and respected. Every person matters and every person is part of our culture of excellence. Building relationships on trust, honesty, and honor are the foundations of the superior culture of excellence of our Punahou boys varsity tennis team. The culture of your team can be whatever you want it to be. Being a true champion in life isn't necessarily all about winning. Yes, it's nice to win, but at the end of the day what's more important is your character as the leader and the character of your team. I know of many business organizations and sports teams that might not be number one in their fields, but whose culture of excellence is highly respected by others. They're definitely viewed as winners. Building champion athletes of character who exhibit integrity and ethics at all times was my top priority and is what I'm most proud of.

To dig deeper, what are the qualities of a champion and a championship team? What standard of excellence do you want your team to have? What qualities do you want your individual team members to possess? What do you want your team to be known for? These are vital questions you need to answer in order to create your own culture of excellence. Such qualities as courage, discipline, humility, cooperation, resiliency, adaptability, loyalty, dedication, positivity, compassion, and self-control are amazing for any team to possess, and it depends on you as the coach to help your team acquire them. It's your job because it's your team. They are a reflection of you! So you, as the coach, had better possess these same qualities as well. Be the example for your team members. Be their inspiration. Be their role model!

As Punahou School's boys varsity tennis coach, I wanted to build the best team that I could build every single year. The way I actually did it was focusing on the well-being of all my team members. I wanted to really understand what was important to them and assist them in accomplishing their personal goals. By communicating and understanding their priorities in life, I could help them make better choices, which would keep them on track towards reaching their goals. It also paid off in that each member knew that I cared first and foremost about him as a person, and second as a tennis player. This became a culture of caring and cohesion in which each team member felt safe and empowered, and I encouraged them to go after anything and everything in life. If you can think it or imagine it, you can achieve it.

You can't have a culture of excellence without teamwork. Helping team members through adversity situations deepens the commitment and trust among team members. Think about an adversity situation of your own and who helped you through it. You probably have deeper trust and commitment with that person who helped you and shared that experience with you. It's the same when you're on a team and you get through a major challenge together. That's why building relationships are powerful. That's why being on a team is powerful. That's why creating a superior culture of excellence is paramount if you want to accomplish anything of significance.

I also wanted to make sure that my team members felt like they could talk with me about any concerns they had. I would give them honest feedback and expected the same from them. In fact, I also advised them that if they came to me with a problem, they should also bring a potential solution to that problem. I wanted them to think about different options and alternatives in finding the best solution possible. As an exercise in role reversal, I also wanted them to think like a head coach or a CEO. Putting themselves in my shoes to see the whole spectrum and view the bigger picture instead of just their part of it often helped them understand my situation in helping both them and the team. In this way, I felt my teams had a bigger appreciation of me as a leader. It really opened their eyes to look at things with a different perspective, so that we had the correct mindset in dealing with challenges together.

After every practice and match competition, I gave my team what I called my "world-famous quote of the day." Having them think about meaningful quotes that would help them in tennis and in life helped reinforce the things that we were working on, and they often remembered these words of wisdom during times of adversity. To this day my former players recite certain "quotes of the day" when we meet. For example, I often shared a quote from Confucius: "Our greatest glory is not in never falling, but in rising every time we fall." Here are some other quotes I shared with my teams:

"A man is a hero not because he is braver than anybody else, but because he is brave for five minutes longer."

"When you want something you've never had, you have to do something you've never done."

"You didn't come this far to come only this far."

"The grass is not always greener on the other side. It's greener where you water it."

"One small crack doesn't mean you're broken. It means you were put to the test and didn't fall apart."

If you come across a quote that resonates with you, I highly encourage you to write it down and share it with your team. You never know when words of wisdom and inspirational sayings will positively impact your team, but I can guarantee it will, sooner or later.

Superior Disciplined Details

There's a tremendous difference between good details and superior disciplined details. Many successful businesses and teams incorporate good details, but truly elite organizations have superior disciplined details. They are very meticulous and never sacrifice quality; good leaders know it's the little things that can separate their team or organization from everyone else. You can have superior disciplined details because it's a choice you can make, it helps raise your standard of excellence, and it's a critical part of your culture.

Let's consider Toyota versus Ferrari and compare these two very different but extremely successful automobile companies. Toyota is the number one selling car in the world—more than ten million a year—and the company boasts a market cap of more than $200 billion. The cars are well made, dependable, safe, and reasonably priced. People who own Toyotas are generally very happy with them. Ferrari, on the other hand, produces only about 8,000 cars each year in order to maintain the exclusivity of the supercar brand. In the interests of exclusivity, Ferrari ideally wants to deliver one less car than the demand, and their supercars are often preordered a year or so in advance. Ferrari is consistently rated as one of the world's most powerful and recognizable brands.

Why is it that when we see a Ferrari on the road, we're captivated and our attention is drawn to it? After all, it's just a car, right? It has four tires and gets you from one place to the next. If you had a choice in owning a Toyota or a Ferrari, which would you choose? This is not a trick question. If the insurance and service visits were completely paid for, which car would you choose? Well, I think you and I would choose the Ferrari in a heartbeat. Ferrari may be in the same automobile market as other successful car manufacturers, but it's in the highest class in a league of its own.

Competitor Lamborghini was founded in 1963, when its founder owned a Ferrari and wanted to build cars to try to exceed the Ferrari's details and style. It is truly a compliment when you set a high standard and others emulate and compete with you to try to surpass your achievements. So what separates Ferrari from all the other automobile companies? Why are these cars so famous and unique and among the most sought-after in the world? It's their superior disciplined details. In addition to their distinctive design and style, they use the finest leather in the world, with each leather seat hand sewn, and the car's meticulous final inspections employ an X-ray machine to identify the smallest cracks or flaws.

The overarching goal is attaining the highest possible standards for quality. The pride and superior details that go into a Ferrari are generally seen as a symbol of speed, wealth, and luxury. For other car companies, a new model often involves just a small redesign with some additional horsepower. For Ferrari, a new model is a new concept with new positioning and completely new technological features. Ferrari consistently pushes for the highest of standards and strives for the highest levels of detailed excellence—both in the cars and from members of the team. There is absolutely nothing wrong with other successful car companies, but we should all be striving for a strong and unique identity like Ferrari's. Because of their superior disciplined details, the company consistently develops the greatest cars in the world and has ultimate pride in its product and its team's culture of excellence.

Bucky Jencks

Having a team first mentality is absolutely necessary. Because tennis is an individual sport like golf, swimming, and track, I wanted everyone on my team to be part of something greater than one person. I wanted the team to be bigger and more important than any one individual, including myself. The only way to put the team first is to make sure that all members feel they're contributing to making the team better and holding each other accountable for every action—or nonaction.

Let me share a story with you. In 2003, a few weeks

before leaving for the state championship on the island of Hawai'i, the top two players on my team were suspended from Punahou School. The school administration informed me that these two were no longer on my team and might possibly be expelled. I had no idea what had happened, but I soon learned that athletes from another school had vandalized the cars of some of our own top athletes. In response, some of the players on our soccer and track teams—as well as my top two players—decided to retaliate. They vandalized the other school by spray-painting graffiti around its campus. Understandably, Punahou School has a zero tolerance policy for situations like these.

So now my team had gone from 12 players to ten in number, and we were on our way to the Big Island. While at the state championship, other teams and coaches were asking my players and me about what had happened. They'd been hearing all kinds of false rumors, and the story was evolving into something far different than what had actually happened. Bucky Jencks, who was number three on my team, instantly stepped up and became a leader. Bucky was a super talented athlete in soccer, track, and tennis. Everyone on our team respected Bucky, an ultimate team player who always put the team first. As a freshman, he won the state doubles championship with his partner, senior Mike Bruggemann. Now as a junior, Bucky found himself on stadium court playing for the state singles championship.

Bucky is a person with extraordinary character and liked by everyone. His opponent from the island of Kaua'i liked and respected him too, but he also defeated Bucky in that championship final. In defeat, Bucky represented our school and team with ultimate class. During the trophy presentation on stadium court, Bucky asked the tournament director if he could use the microphone to address the crowd. First, he congratulated his opponent for winning and playing incredible tennis. Second, he thanked the tournament director, umpires, volunteers, fans, and all the families there supporting their sons and daughters. Third, Bucky said, "I want to address the

Bucky Jencks

unfortunate incidents you're probably aware of between a few athletes from Punahou and another school. Their actions are unacceptable. It's a reflection of a few students who made a poor choice. It's not a reflection of the entire school. As I hope you saw in this tournament, my teammates and I represented our school and families to the best of our abilities. This is who Punahou School is, and this is who we are as Punahou students. Please don't let the unfortunate actions of a handful of students taint your view of us or our school."

Upon handing the microphone back to the tournament director, Bucky received major applause and a standing ovation from everyone there. His meaningful words provided much needed clarity. Players from the other school involved in the incident approached our boys and girls varsity players to shake hands and hug. It was such a beautiful thing to see. Out of a thoughtless, stupid choice of a few came a closer bond of respect and appreciation between players representing both schools. Needless to say, I was so proud of Bucky for being proactive and doing what he did. By putting his team first, he not only united every school and athlete, he consequently held himself, our team, and everyone there to an even higher standard of excellence.

Robbie Lim

In my book *Beyond the Lines*, I shared Robbie Lim's story, but only through his junior year in high school. Here's what happened the following year. In 2004 Robbie was the two-time state singles champion and captain of our Punahou boys varsity team, and what an incredible captain he was. He continued to help and nurture his teammates, partly by reciting inspirational quotes from well-known movies, which would motivate everyone—including me. Robbie had a lot of fun and gave 1,000 percent effort all the time. Practices and matches were all the same to him. That's how the mindset is with champions.

After going undefeated during the regular season, Robbie won our league tournament, earning him the number one seed for the state championship on the Big Island. When Robbie won the state championship as a sophomore, two of his opponents had had issues with cramping. In his junior year, Robbie and his opponent both suffered major cramping in the quarterfinals, but Robbie persevered through these unforgettable matches to win his second state singles championship. Now a senior and two-time state champion, Robbie was definitely favored to win again.

Robbie Lim

If you know anything about the weather in Hawai'i, you know it can get extremely hot during the month of May on the island of Hawai'i. Having my team members properly hydrated was a definite priority. In fact, I had them drink extra water starting one full week before we left O'ahu for the Big Island. As prepared as we were, it was still guaranteed to feel like an oven and everyone would need to deal with it.

Our team clinched the state team championship on the second day, and we were all looking forward to the semifinals and finals on the third day. Robbie matched up against the top player from the Big Island, who had a very strong serve and a powerful all-court game. As for me, I was planning ahead, thinking of what Robbie needed to do in the semifinals under the extremely hot condition. I expected he would win and then have a one-hour rest period before playing the championship final.

I wanted to make sure he would give it his best and earn a third singles title. In order for Robbie to have that opportunity, we focused on our strategy and how well he could execute it. I told Robbie that this semifinal was going to be a tough match, that there was a hard way of winning and a smart way of winning. The hard way would be for Robbie to play a three-hour match using his usual aggressive baseline game to wear down and ultimately break his opponent physically and mentally. The problem would be that he'd most likely win but then have no gas left in the tank for the championship final. The smart way would be for Robbie to play shorter points by taking advantage of midcourt balls and attacking the net as soon as possible. In this way, he would still likely win the semifinal match but would have more gas in that tank for the final.

I went over these two strategy options with Robbie and told him it was up to him to make a choice and live with the consequences. Robbie went out on the court and gave his usual 1,000 percent effort and competed with class. I was so proud watching him. However, he was doing it the hard way. It was like a heavyweight boxing match, and both players exchanged major blows with their powerful groundstrokes. It was a grueling match for both players. Robbie won 7–6, 7–5 but the match lasted three hours. The other semifinal, meanwhile, lasted barely an hour. Robbie had one hour to rest and recover while his opponent had three.

In matches, Robbie was always very prepared and better hydrated than most. Most players will have a water jug or a small cooler with water and Gatorade. Not Robbie. He had one of those big family-size coolers loaded with water, Gatorade, fruits, and enough drinks for an entire team. And the funny thing is, he would have two of the younger players on the team carry it out onto the court for him.

Despite the grueling heat and his short break, Robbie seemed to be recovering well before the championship match. I was still very concerned that he'd expended too much energy in the earlier match and might not have enough left to go the distance. After reviewing our strategy with him, I looked at

Robbie and said, "Who's the champ?" He looked at me with confidence and replied, "Coach, I'm the champ!" I responded, "Go get 'em, champ!" We both smiled as he walked onto the court, knowing that this was the final tennis match of his high school career.

His opponent was a tough competitor and another very strong player from the Big Island. I knew there was nothing further I could do to prepare Robbie for this occasion. Now it was all up to him to compete and execute. And compete and execute is what he did. Robbie was playing brilliant tennis. His serves were strong, his groundstrokes powerful, his strategy effective, and all this performed with a determined mindset. Robbie dominated and won the first set 6-1.

I walked onto the court for our two-minute coaching break and told Robbie to keep his focus, play one point at a time, and stay committed to our strategy. Because of the heat and the amount of energy he had expended in the semifinal, Robbie's only hope was to play shorter points and attack the net as soon as the opportunity presented itself. Yes, this was the "smart way"—very similar to how I'd wanted him to play in the semifinal. I felt good seeing that he'd also committed to this strategy in the final. As the umpire yelled out, "Time," I hugged Robbie, telling him how proud I was and that this was likely the last time I'd be coaching him. Robbie responded, "Coach, you're the champ!"

Robbie began serving the second set with a strong, focused mindset and continued to execute our strategy flawlessly. He was controlling the points with his heavy topspin groundstrokes, taking advantage of every midcourt shot and finishing off the point with his volley or overhead. It was total dominance and every spectator could see why Robbie was a champion. But with a 3–1 lead in the second set, Robbie took an unusual amount of extra time before serving the next game. He looked over at me and I knew something was wrong.

Immediately after giving me that look, Robbie fell to the ground with extremely painful cramps in both legs. The umpire called a medical time-out and I ran onto the court, where

Robbie was screaming in pain. I mean he was screaming! The pain was so severe that we moved him into a shaded area next to the court. As we tried to keep the spectators away, Robbie began experiencing full body cramps and the screaming grew even louder. After five minutes of agony, the umpire said that Robbie needed to get back onto the court to continue playing or retire the match.

"Robbie," I said, "this is bad. I mean really bad. We need to retire the match."

"Coach, I want to get back on the court and try," he told me.

"Robs, I know you can be stubborn in a good way, but this is being stubborn in a bad way. Let's retire the match. There's no way you'll be able to finish in this condition."

"Coach, please let me just try one more time."

"You know that I'm more concerned about you and your health rather than a tennis match, right?"

Robbie nodded and again said, "Let me try one more time."

I stepped aside and Robbie grabbed his tennis racket and slowly hobbled back onto the court towards the baseline to serve. With a 3–1 lead in the set, he was only three games away and probably needed just ten more minutes to win the match. Still in obvious pain, Robbie hit the softest serve I've ever seen in my life and couldn't move two steps to play the next shot. The exact same thing happened on the next point. Before serving the third point, Robbie again looked at me and then fell to the ground. The cramps were back along with the screaming.

I ran onto the court and he hobbled his way towards the back fence to pick up his towel. He covered his head with the towel, crying. I started crying too. I lifted up one end of the towel, and then we were both under there crying together.

I said, "Champ, that's it. I told the umpire as I ran out here that you're done, that we retire."

"Coach, I don't want to give up. I never give up. I don't want to let my teammates down and I don't want to let you down."

"Robs, the whole team and I are so proud of you. This is not giving up. You gave everything you had, and there's nothing left to give. We're calling an ambulance to take you to the hospital."

Then our entire team gathered around him and everyone congratulated Robbie for giving everything he had. The paramedics came soon after to walk him slowly to the ambulance.

After I talked with his parents, Richard and Carin Lim, it was determined that Robbie wouldn't return on the flight with the team. He'd be treated with IVs at the hospital and would probably take an evening flight back to O'ahu. I gathered my team together and we left the tennis club and headed to the Kona Airport.

Once we checked in and cleared security, we all sat down together in the restaurant and digested everything that happened earlier. I listened to the guys talk about how impressed they were with their captain. They were inspired watching how Robbie gave everything he had, and they were missing him because he wasn't going home with us. As I listened to these priceless comments, my phone rang.

The call was from a nurse back at the hospital. "Coach Rusty," she said, "your player Robbie is very stubborn. He wants to leave the hospital and get to the airport in time to travel back with the team."

"He's stubborn, all right," I answered, "but hopefully he's recovering and feeling better there with you."

"He left ten minutes ago," she said. "He's coming to meet you there."

I shook my head and thought to myself, *That's Robbie!* I didn't tell any of the guys that their captain was on his way because I wanted to see their reaction. Twenty minutes later Robbie walked into the restaurant with tears in his eyes. His teammates, also teary eyed, were super excited to see him, and they all hugged him and told him how proud they were of him. It brought tears to my eyes, and it was clear to me that this was about much more than just playing tennis. This was the superior culture of excellence of our tennis team. 🎾

6 KEYS FOR PEAK PERFORMANCE

---◆---

"Start by doing what's necessary, then what's possible,
and suddenly you are doing the impossible."
—Francis of Assisi

CHAPTER 6

KEY NO. 1: PHYSICAL

> *"You can practice shooting eight hours a day, but if your technique is wrong, then all you become is very good at shooting the wrong way. Get the fundamentals down and the level of everything you do will rise."*
> —Michael Jordan

The physical key deals with how good you are at physically doing your job in two situations: you as an individual and you with your team. You are a reflection of your team, and your team is a reflection of you. If you're leading a business team, how good are you physically at doing your job? If you're coaching a sports team, how good are you as a coach? What would you rate yourself on a scale of one to ten? Now, what would you rate your team on a scale of one to ten? These are two different yet important situations for you to reflect on. The point is this: You are responsible for you, and you are responsible for your team.

There's a gigantic difference in being a great person and a great leader. As I mentioned earlier, there are many coaches and CEOs who have the right principles, values, and disciplines for themselves and they might even be extraordinary as an individual, but they might struggle in transferring those same principles, values, and disciplines to their team. I've seen this happen a ton with people in leadership positions who deeply care about their team and just need help coaching them in a better, more effective way.

Hit It In

In soccer, you need to score goals. In basketball, you need to shoot baskets. In tennis, you need to hit it in! It's all about fundamentals. The physical fundamentals you and your team have are the foundations necessary to give your team a chance to succeed. In business, how good are your frontline team members in dealing with current and potential clients? Are they speaking with them in a professional and caring way? Do they have great communication skills? Are they offering different options and solutions to solve problems? These are some examples of basic fundamentals for any successful business. Or, are they making careless mistakes? And, do these mistakes happen often? Are there complaints from clients because of how your frontline team members spoke to them? Are you losing clients? Is there dysfunction among team members? It's your responsibility as the leader to coach your team members properly. They're a reflection of you!

Focusing on the basics and keeping things simple is paramount. My players would frequently hear me say the words "hit it in" before stepping on the tennis court for a big match. Let's think about it. In tennis, you have to hit it in to win. You cannot hit it out and win. Hitting the ball in one more time than your opponent gives you that chance to win. You might hit it high or low, or hard or soft. Whatever you do, if you want to win, hit it in. There are only two ways to win a point in tennis: you hit a winner, or your opponent makes an error. It's as simple as that. So I pose this question to my players: "Is it easier to hit winners on every point or for our opponent to make errors?" They all agree that we might hit some winners, but the majority of points we win will be because our opponent makes errors because of our solid performance. And, it's true that most teams achieve victory not because of the big plays they make, but because of the errors they don't make.

Now, think about your own team in business or sports. What are the most basic fundamentals you need to do to give your team a chance to succeed? Sometimes things become complicated and seem to evolve into unnecessary complex situations. Your job as the leader is to make certain that everything is kept simple and clear. If you don't, it often leads your team members to feel overwhelmed, assuring that they will definitely not perform anywhere close to their potential.

Let me explain this concept even further. How do we hit it in? Where do we aim our shots? There are two things that make tennis challenging: the net and the lines. It's unbelievable to me when I see players aiming one inch over the net or trying to hit it two inches from the lines, and then getting upset when they miss. I'll ask them, "Can you hit that shot in ten times out of ten? Of course not! If you're that risky you're probably going to miss more shots than you make. You might make three out of ten but is that a good percentage to help you win?"

Another thing that I would often say is "big shot, big target." What I mean by this is I want my player to be aggressive and confident when going for our big shots, but I want them to aim those shots to a big area on the court. I would often say, "Aim for a big target area instead of a small target area and we will hit it in a lot." The tennis professionals on TV do this same thing all the time. It's relevant no matter what level of player you are. This is a very basic, yet valuable concept and completely relates to anything you are striving to achieve. This is an example of how I kept things simple with advanced players and you can do the same with your team. Strip it down to the basics and always remember the most important fundamentals that your team needs to do that will lead to success.

Climb the Mountain

We had great structure in our tennis practices and I had my team doing many things that our competitors were not doing. Before every practice, we would do various stretches together as a team. We would then go over to the school track for a variety of running exercises to help improve the aerobic part of tennis, then to the steep hill near our tennis courts to sprint up the incline and jog down (eight to 12 times at varying distances). These things were done before my players even picked up their tennis rackets to begin hitting balls on the court.

In order to enhance what we did on the court, I needed my players to get tougher and stronger physically off the court. When some players start a tennis match, they're often playing very strong through the first set and usually midway through the second, before fatigue sets in and they begin to run out of gas. This obviously affects their performance, focus, and consistency. I wanted my players to finish the match as strong as they started it. When I required my players to get in the gym, lifting weights two times a week, it not only helped them physically, it helped them mentally. They knew they were doing more than their competitors and felt like they deserved to win. That feeling of deserving to win is a powerful one. I was also mindful that their first priority as students is school and helped them learn time management. They had a demanding school schedule but everyone can make time to exercise 15 or 20 minutes on a given day by planning ahead. Depending on their schedule, our players would get in the gym for 15 minutes to an hour to do their workouts. Now, even if they had time constraints and could only do the minimum time commitment, a lot of these 15-minute workouts led to many extra hours of preparation. By physically improving our conditioning, footwork, strength, flexibility, and balance, it greatly enhanced how we performed on the tennis court, giving my players opportunities for peak performance.

Think about what you are currently doing physically with your people in your business or on your team. Now think about ways to enhance this physical part. How can you make them stronger and better so that they can attain peak performance throughout the entire day? What can you do to ensure they can go from one task to the next without getting fatigued? It's important in everything you do to start strong and to finish strong. You should be able to complete your last task of the day as well as you did the first one. If you work hard and smart, doing more than others are doing will give you an edge. How amazing is the feeling you get when you go on a hike and reach the top of the mountain? Well, when you start the hike, the goal is to make it to the top. Not just halfway or a hundred yards away. Get there. Go all the way! Everyone feels challenged physically. It takes relentless perseverance to achieve your goal and make it to the top of the mountain. And once you're there, how awesome is the view and feeling of accomplishment? So climb that mountain and do what many others don't.

Take the Punches

How much can you physically endure? How many punches can you take? Anyone can throw them, but not everyone can handle being punched. In boxing or mixed martial arts, you never know when you're one punch away from winning or getting knocked out. The only way to get tougher and better is to put yourself through adversity and uncomfortable situations. Think about it. It might not be easy at first, but if you're prepared and ready to rise to the challenge, you can handle the punches. By dealing with it, you actually become stronger, tougher, and better from that experience.

When you set a goal and want to achieve something of significance, it rarely comes easy. I used to share a story with my players about traveling. If I'm taking a trip from Honolulu to New York (with a connecting flight in Dallas), there are certain challenges that might arise. After arriving at the airport, there might be a long line at check-in and another long line going through security. Once on the plane, there might be an unexpected delay even before takeoff. Once we're in the air, there could be an unreasonable, disruptive passenger giving headaches to the flight attendants, as well the rest of us. We also might experience turbulence and strong headwinds. Once we arrive in Dallas, we might have only ten minutes to make our connecting flight, only to find that the gate is in the next terminal. After barely making it on the connecting flight, there might be another delay because the pilots need the mechanics to check something in the plane. Once we're in the air, it's a smooth flight until we experience turbulence again and, with some severe crosswinds upon landing, finally arrive in New York.

How much adversity can you really handle in reaching your destination? How much can you tolerate in striving to accomplish your goal? How many unfortunate situations can you deal with and still stay positive? How many roadblocks can you overcome? The most successful leaders and teams stay fixated on their destination and are determined to succeed no matter how tough the challenges might be to get there. They can take multiple punches because they are resilient and have relentless perseverance in achieving their goal. I have found that if you want something badly enough, you will adjust, redirect, and find a way.

Mikey Lim and Skyler Tateishi

In 2006, I had a player named Mikey Lim, Robbie's younger brother by two years, who won the state singles championship in his junior year. Now he was a senior, team captain, and the number one player on our team, and I wanted him to help me build the confidence of junior Skyler Tateishi. Skyler was number two on our team and I knew the following year he would most likely be number one after Mikey graduated. Mikey and Skyler were the top two players on the team by far. I talked with Mikey and asked him to take Skyler under his wing and help him develop as much as possible through the season. Being the great team player he is, Mikey agreed without hesitation. Skyler looked up to Mikey, and I knew they would push one another, ultimately helping the other player improve.

Mikey Lim and Skyler Tateishi

Through the season, it was amazing to see how much Mikey was helping Skyler. It was inspiring the other junior and senior players on our team to help mentor the freshmen and sophomores. As a coach, I loved seeing this. The younger players were getting more confident in themselves and the upperclassmen felt great, knowing that these younger teammates were the ones who'd be filling their shoes next year or the year after. It was like I had multiple assistants all working towards the same goal.

Once the regular season finished, we were ready for our league championship tournament. Mikey was the number one seed and Skyler number two. Yes, you can already guess what happened. They both got through their draws, made it to the singles championship, and ended up playing against each other. Through the season, Mikey had always beat Skyler in practice matches. But, on this occasion, anything could happen.

I sat in the front row on the bleachers next to the 'Iolani School athletic director, who observed that this should really be the state championship final. I agreed with him. They were battling and the level of play was incredibly high. They were hitting powerful groundstrokes with very few unforced errors. Towards the end of the third set, the match was nearing the three-hour mark. It was so close and exciting, and I still had no idea who would win. They both gave it their all and it literally came down to one or two points, which really came down to one or two shots. Skyler seized the opportunity, took a chance, executed, and won. As he walked to the net to shake hands with Mikey, Skyler looked like he was half excited and half sad. He respected Mikey greatly and it was the first time he had beaten him. For his part, Mikey looked like he was genuinely happy for Skyler and extremely sad and disappointed at the same time.

On the ride home, I asked Mikey what his thoughts were and the first thing he said was, "Wow! Skyler played awesome. He was tough!"

"Yep! You helped make him tough."

Mikey went on to say how happy he was for Skyler to break through and win the league championship. He also said that he was disappointed in himself for not being able to find a way to win and missing some key shots on big points. I told Mikey how proud I was of both of them as I watched the match, and that it was sad that somebody had to lose. As happy as he was for his teammate, I could sense that he was beginning to feel really bummed.

Mikey had been last year's state singles champion, seeded number one in the league championship, and lost to the teammate that I'd asked him to take under his wing. "If you could choose between winning the league championship or the state championship in two weeks," I asked him, "which would you choose?"

"The state championship, of course."

"There you go!" I said. "This is a good wake-up call for you. Sometimes a tough loss like this is a blessing in disguise. If you won today, you might assume that everything is OK with your game. But after this loss, you'll focus on those details that you need to polish up. What's done is done. That loss is in the past. Focus on improving every part of your game in the next two weeks and continue to help Skyler and he'll be helping you as well."

Mikey agreed and when he left, he said simply, "Thanks, Coach!"

I could see that he had the right mindset and was fully committed to improving himself, Skyler, and the rest of our team. Our team practices resumed a few days later in preparation for the state championship on Oʻahu and it was intense and a whole lot of fun. When the tournament began, Mikey was there watching and cheering on Skyler in all of his matches, and Skyler did the same for Mikey. The support they showed to each other and their teammates was wonderful to see. That's what a real team is all about. As it turned out, Skyler lost in the semifinals and Mikey went on to win his semifinal match on the other side of the draw. And yes, Mikey dominated the final, winning his second state singles championship. The following year, a confident Skyler was extremely dominant, winning the state singles championship, and I clearly remember Mikey calling him on the phone from college to congratulate him. They were both outstanding champions and very selfless, which became contagious with their teammates for years to come. 🎾

CHAPTER 7

KEY NO. 2: MENTAL

*"Focus on the possibilities for success,
not on the potential for failure."*
—Napoleon Hill

The mental key deals with how good you are at focusing and concentrating on your job and completing your tasks. Noise and distractions are things that people with average mental focus experience. Great leaders with exceptional mental focus can block out any noise and distractions to complete the task at hand. Think about when you're at a restaurant in a conversation with someone and the waiter drops a stack of plates and glasses across the way—do you look? Or do you continue on with your conversation as if nothing happened? The common response is to look and see what happened. But, if you're extremely focused, nothing will disrupt or deter you from the task at hand.

The great Dallas Cowboys football coach Tom Landry said, "There is only a half step difference between the champions and those who finish on the bottom. And much of that half step is mental." I completely agree. Time and time again I've seen how little the differences are between being a champion and being a finalist. It's consistently having the right mental frame of mind and the ability to focus on the here and now.

Mental Toughness

In my youth, I would often hear people say that sports is 90 percent mental and ten percent physical. I think that's probably true in most of the things we do in life. Having the right mindset and perspective makes all the difference. All successful leaders and teams have mental toughness. You've heard those two words before but what exactly is it? Mental toughness is the ability to create and maintain the right kind of internal feeling, regardless of the circumstances. The brain controls the body so controlling your thoughts and having the right internal climate gives you the opportunity for peak performance.

It doesn't matter if a bad call is made against you and you feel cheated. It doesn't matter if you receive bad news and feel disappointed. It doesn't matter if you get injured and feel frustrated. We've all experienced these situations in life. What matters is how you respond. Are you resilient? Can you have present focus instead of worrying about the past or the future? Do you have mental toughness? In tennis, I would share with my players that we need our physical toughness to weaken our opponent in a match, and our mental toughness will make them crack, causing us to win. Our opponent might be able to match us physically, but we might have the clear advantage mentally.

Owning mental toughness builds the foundations for long-term success and it's a choice you can make for yourself. Former Navy SEAL commander Jocko Willink said, "If you want to be tougher mentally, it is simple: Be tougher. Don't meditate on it." I completely agree with him. If you want to be tougher, then be tougher. It's really a simple decision. It's very recognizable and obvious to identify teams that are mentally tough. These teams made the conscious decision to be mentally tough, which becomes a habit, and part of their identity.

Master Your Mindset

Having the right perspective in looking forward to challenges and welcoming adversity is absolutely necessary. It's a mindset. What do you think is the mindset of champions? How much adversity do you think championship teams can tolerate? How much can you tolerate? They always look forward to adversity and rise to all challenges. If you're doing a long-distance run with a friend and you begin to feel tired and a bit exhausted, do you stop or do you keep going? If you're weight lifting in the gym and feel fatigued, do you quit or keep pushing through it? We've all had these thoughts and experiences because we're human. But if every day matters, we need to keep improving ourselves and overcome these daily challenges all the time. Not just sometimes. All the time! This needs to become a habit. In order for it to become a habit, you need to look forward to your next challenging experience and view it as an opportunity to improve yourself. Use your new and improved mental toughness and you'll have a great sense of accomplishment when you get through it.

One way to guarantee success is to have the mindset that success is never owned—it is rented and the rent is due every day. If you earn a number one ranking in business, you have achieved success. But how do you sustain success? You can win a championship today but it doesn't guarantee that you will win a championship again in the future. It's what you do every day that assures success for you and your team. It's a mindset that you need to have to keep moving your team forward in the right direction. After winning or achieving something significant, ask your team, "How can we outdo what we've done? What can we do to be better today than we were yesterday?" Professional sports teams study films of games they've played to review things that worked and what didn't work. They also study films of their next opponent to learn as much as they can in order to be as prepared as possible. They're willing to take time and focus on the details to make success more likely.

Mastering your mindset will give you confidence to achieve anything you're aiming for. It's conditioning your mind to know that you can accomplish anything you set your mind to, to ignore the doubters and disregard people who are pessimistic and negative. It's you consistently focusing on encouraging yourself and being optimistic. It's your inner voice saying, "I can do it, and I will."

Prioritize Your Priorities

When you wake up in the morning, the first thing you should think about is asking yourself three important questions: Who do I love? What do I love? What do I love about myself? The reason is it immediately puts you in the right mindset by being thankful and grateful for everyone and everything you have in your life, and you begin your day with a positive attitude. Because we lead busy lives, if we don't reflect on these important questions we can be easily sidetracked into feeling stressed and negative about the things that lie ahead. This is a very critical habit to own because it keeps you focused on the big picture of life instead of getting irritated and frustrated about petty things that occur throughout the day. This mindset and routine will keep you centered in striving to take care of the people and achieve the tasks that are most important to you.

When you're able to prioritize your priorities, it keeps you on track to achieving your goals. Some people have so many things on their to-do list that they rarely make a dent in it. Investor and philanthropist Warren Buffet has a simple three-step process for this. First, he'll write down a list of his top 25 goals. Second, he'll circle the five most important goals. Third, he'll cross off and completely eliminate the other 20 goals, even if they're somewhat important to him. Buffett's reasoning is that those 20 goals are lower in priority and actually take away his energy and focus in achieving the top five priorities. The only way to accomplish your top five goals is to put all your effort, energy, and focus into them. The other goals are actually distractions that inhibit you from accomplishing your most important goals.

Ross Inouye

During my first season as head coach in 1994, I had a senior on my team named Ross Inouye, who was ranked number one in the boys 18 division in the state of Hawai'i. He had great character, was highly respected and liked by everyone. Once our season finished, Ross asked me if I could train him

Ross Inouye

in private tennis lessons to prepare him for tryouts at Stanford University in the fall. We set up a schedule where I could train him three times a week during the summer—twice in private lessons and once in an advanced group training session.

Ross's goal was to make the Stanford tennis team, which was the top college team in the United States. Ross had won hundreds of matches because he was a very consistent player, but we needed him to be more aggressive and add more power to have a chance to compete at that level in college. As an incoming freshman, he could be playing against men three or four years older than he was, and therefore we needed to raise his level of play quickly. The transition from high school to college is challenging in academics, but even more so in athletics. Ross trusted me and was fully committed to working on improving these parts of his game for the next three months.

Once the Stanford tennis tryouts concluded, Ross called me on the phone and said that he has good news and bad news. I didn't know what to think but I asked him to give me the good news first.

"Coach, I beat a couple of nationally ranked players in tryouts and the good news is I finished at number 12."

"That's great news, Ross! Stanford has so much team depth and outstanding players from top to bottom. Finishing at number 12 is a fantastic accomplishment. What's the bad news?"

"The bad news is the coach said they're keeping only ten players on the team this year."

I couldn't believe it. I felt devastated, as though I was the one who didn't make the team. I could only imagine what Ross was thinking and feeling.

I said, "Ross, I'm so sorry. We had prepared you and you worked so hard these past few months, sacrificing other things in order to get your tennis game to that next level. How are you and what are you thinking?"

"Coach, I'm OK. When I come home during Christmas break, can you train me in privates and group again? I want to keep working on my game through this year, train with you all summer, and try out for the team again next year."

"Yes, you know I'll help you any way I can. But, what if the same result happens?"

"It very well could, but if there's a chance I can make the team, I want to take that chance. I'm so close and I know I can do it."

When Ross was a sophomore, he called me again on the last day of tryouts. "Coach," he said, "I have good news and bad news."

I said, "Not again! You're killing me, Ross! Tell me the good news."

"Well, I played awesome in the challenge matches, beating a bunch of nationally ranked players, and the good news is I finished tryouts at number nine."

"Don't tell me the coach is only keeping eight players!" I said. "What's the bad news?"

"Coach, there is no bad news. They're keeping ten players. I'm on the team!"

I said, "Ross, I am so happy and very proud of you. I feel like I made the team too! Your mindset and commitment through this year, having a goal and going after it no matter the odds, is truly admirable and extremely inspirational."

"Thanks, Coach," he replied. "Thanks for helping me and believing in me. I couldn't have done it without you."

Ross was on the Stanford tennis team for three years and has two national championship rings. By the way, while he was there, a guy by the name of Tiger Woods was on the Stanford golf team and many of the golf and tennis players were good friends with each other. Ross's accomplishment is tremendously inspiring because of his mental focus in going after something that is important to him. I am so grateful that I was a part of this priceless experience for him, and I've shared this story with countless players over the years to inspire them and give them hope to go after anything they want in life. 🎾

---◆---

CHAPTER 8

KEY NO. 3: EMOTIONAL

"Emotions can get in the way or get you on the way."
—Mavis Mazhura

The emotional key deals with how good you are at controlling your emotions and being aware of the emotions of others. Some people make irrational decisions because of how they feel at that moment. It's definitely good to show your passion if you're able to control your emotions. The greatest leaders always make decisions based on reason, not emotion. Coaching your team to be aware when people become emotional and taking some time afterwards to recover from that experience allows them to control themselves and the situation in a positive way. Remember, you always need to control the situation instead of having the situation control you. Having emotional awareness is necessary for you and your team to have peak performance.

Attitude vs. Mood

Don't be confused between attitude and mood. A mood is a reflection of your attitude. If you change your attitude, you can change your mood. People with a poor attitude often end up with a bad mood. Others with a positive attitude often experience good moods. That's the power of your attitude and keeping a positive perspective and outlook in life. Anger, frustration, and depression are a mindset, which is often temporary but it could evolve into a bad habit and affect your lifestyle. A positive attitude allows a chain of events to happen. It leads to having happy thoughts, favorable experiences, good feelings, better results, and winning. Now think about what would happen if you would have a bad attitude right now. How will that negativity affect your mood, feelings, thoughts, experiences, results, and your life?

In order to have emotional toughness, you need to control your attitude and keep it positive all the time. It needs to become a habit. When it becomes a habit, you will have control over your thoughts and control over your life. You will then be able to control your destiny and accomplish extraordinary results. Nobody wants to hang around with negative, hopeless people. So listen to me right now and don't be one of those people.

The legendary actor Morgan Freeman said, "Self-control is strength. Calmness is mastery. You have to get to a point where your mood doesn't shift based on the insignificant actions of someone else. Don't allow others to control the direction of your life. Don't allow your emotions to overpower your intelligence."

Being aware and sensing when others around you are having negative emotions allows you the opportunity to help them. You can be the sunshine on their cloudy day. In order to achieve goals or anything significant in life depends on your perspective towards it. Keeping a positive outlook keeps you on the right track. No one has ever won a championship by being grumpy, depressed, and negative. If you like losing and failure, choose a bad attitude. If you want to win and achieve greatness, choose a positive one.

New Experiences, New Feelings

If you don't try anything new, everything in your life will stay the same. A parent who exposes their son or daughter to a variety of sports and activities allows their child the opportunity to try new things to see what they like and don't like. It gives them the chance to have new experiences in the hope that they will find something they are passionate about and truly love. The same is true about relationships. A man or woman looking for a soul mate will not find one by staying at home. They need to go out to different places and meet new people. If you haven't found love with a partner, you definitely won't find them by staying at home and being isolated. Opening up yourself to new experiences gives you opportunities to meet different people, experience new feelings, and live a better, more fulfilled life.

When you have these new experiences, it leads to an entire spectrum of new feelings. The more experiences you have, the better. Feeling the width and depth of various emotions will ultimately help you in your life and you will be able to help many others. Many of us have experienced the thrill of victory as well as the agony of defeat. Experiencing the agony makes us appreciate the victories even more. It's about the highs and the lows. You appreciate winning even more after some tough emotional defeats. These experiences ultimately make you a better, tougher, and stronger person for going through difficult adversities in life.

Some years ago, my friend Reynold and his wife, Allison, wanted a Maltese puppy and found a breeder who had a litter of three male pups. After selecting one and calling me on the phone with excitement, they suggested that I go look at the puppies as well. I went the next day and one of the two puppies was extra happy to see me, kissing me and showing me lots of attention. He basically chose me and there's no way I could have said no—they are so adorable!

When I was able to bring him home a week later, I named him Ace (yes, an obvious tennis connection) and had watched all of Cesar Millan's videos the week prior to prepare me for this big commitment—as it wasn't just about me anymore. I wanted to care for Ace in the best possible way and give him a happy, healthy life. Ace would go everywhere with me and because of his lovable personality, he made lots of friends— both dogs and humans.

Three years later on a regular doggie checkup, the vet told me that Ace had a heart murmur we needed to keep an eye on. I was definitely concerned upon hearing the news, but Ace seemed as happy as ever, looking forward to our daily adventures. He loved hiking, car rides, going to the beach, and of course, playing with his doggie friends. One day after I'd finished private tennis lessons with my students, I noticed that Ace's breathing seemed a little different. He usually ran up the stairs, but this time he waited at the bottom for me to carry him up. This was very odd, and later that night his breathing seemed more exaggerated. In the morning, I took him to the vet, who told me to give Ace medicine only after eating. Well, this was the first time that Ace hadn't had an appetite and had eaten nothing, which meant that I couldn't give him the medicine. That night his breathing worsened and, extremely worried, I took him to the emergency pet hospital. The doctor immediately put Ace in an oxygen chamber, with a diagnosis of possible pneumonia. I was told they'd keep Ace with them that day and overnight to monitor his breathing. I was to go home, and that no news from them would be good news for me.

At my condo, hoping and praying for the best, I watched as time passed from 8 p.m. to 9 p.m. and then to 10 p.m. I'd received no call from the doctor and began to feel a bit relieved and hopeful that Ace was experiencing a relatively normal sickness and was on his way to a full recovery. I dozed off and my phone rang at 1 a.m.

"Rusty!" the doctor said. "We need you to come to the hospital right away! Ace took a turn for the worse and died, but we performed CPR and now he's come back."

When I arrived at the hospital, the doctor took me in the back to see Ace. He was lying on his side, unconscious, with a tube in his mouth, and was breathing extremely heavily. His eyes were open and I knew he knew I was there with him. I was crying and kissing his face hoping that this was just a bad dream. The doctor consoled me, saying how rare it was for a dog to come back after CPR. I was so happy and grateful that he had! And then the doctor said, "Ace came back to say goodbye to you." Soon after, the beeps on the machine began to slow, Ace's eyes began to close, and he passed away.

It was the absolute worst feeling I've ever had in my life. I felt like I lost a part of my heart that day, and that missing part will never be replaced. I miss Ace tremendously and think about him every day. My years with him were the happiest years of my life. It's incredible how a dog can mean so much. Bringing him home that first time was the best decision I've ever made. He taught me deeper meanings about enthusiasm (because he was always so happy to see me), loyalty, caring, and love. Even though losing him was the worst feeling I've ever experienced, the joy and happiness I had with Ace was truly priceless. So believe me when I encourage you to experience new things, because they can give you the chance to grow and discover powerful new emotions that will stimulate your life in unimaginable ways.

Kevin Caulfield

A player who has passion, listens well, and works hard is someone any coach would love to have. In addition, a player with amazing quickness and footwork, great shot consistency, and high intelligence makes that player even more valuable to a team. That's the kind of player Kevin Caulfield was to our team. By his senior year, he had been voted captain and was our number one player. He had big respect from his teammates and competitors because of his strong mind and great physical toughness on the tennis court. If I'm being really picky and critical, Kevin had only one weakness—his emotional responses to certain players.

Now let me convey this clearly so that you completely understand. Kevin had emotional toughness most of the time, but one particular competitor from Maryknoll School, who was a year older than Kevin, could really rattle his emotions. He seemed like a nice boy off the tennis court, but on the

Kevin Caulfield (right) with Skyler Tateishi

court he behaved differently and would get under Kevin's skin. I mean his behavior was really bad. He would cheat on purpose by making bad line calls. He would question every line call Kevin made. He would ask what the score was after Kevin called the score aloud. He wouldn't give the balls nicely to Kevin in between points. And he would call Kevin names that weren't nice. I believe he did all of these unsportsmanlike things because he wanted to win at all costs. Now put yourself in Kevin's shoes. Who wouldn't get irritated and frustrated with an opponent like this?

During Kevin's junior year, he played this boy twice in the regular season, winning one and losing one. This boy was a really good player who didn't have to resort to this type of behavior to win matches. In fact, I believe he could have been an even greater player and competed at a much higher level had he behaved properly and respected the etiquette of tennis. But his unacceptable behavior greatly affected Kevin and how he competed against him. Kevin was well aware that the Maryknoll player pulled these antics just to irritate him, and everyone watching could clearly see the effects they had on him. This kept Kevin from playing up to his full potential and made him more vulnerable to defeat.

At the state championship in Wailea, Maui, Kevin and this boy won their early round matches and would compete against each other in the quarterfinals. I knew Kevin felt uneasy going into this match because he already knew he was about to be treated badly yet again. So the key was to get Kevin in the right mindset, to totally control his emotions from the first serve until match point, something that he hadn't been able to do in previous matches. We already knew all of his opponent's tricks, so we knew what to expect. My challenge was finding the most effective way to help Kevin deal with it.

"This boy has tried every trick in the book against you," I told Kevin, "so the good news is we know what to expect. The bad news is I don't know how you'll respond. You know he does those things because he knows he can't beat you without them. People like that want to get a reaction from you. They see how their action affects you in a negative way. That's why they do it. My challenge to you in this match is to be 'cool as ice.' Show no emotion. Let him do what he'll do and show him that nothing affects you. If you can do this, it will drive him nuts. The spectators will see how bad his attitude and behavior really is, and I have no doubt that you will win."

"Coach, that makes complete sense. And you're right, I haven't been able to control my emotions against him for an entire match."

"Kevin, I know you can do it and I know you love a challenge. And think about this—this is the last time you'll ever play against him because he's a senior. And if you beat him, his high school tennis career is over. Wouldn't that feel sweet and amazing?" I looked into Kevin's eyes and I could see an aura of calm intensity within—he would rise to this challenge.

"Coach," he said, "I'm ready."

I felt proud watching Kevin walk onto the court and even

prouder watching him compete. Sure enough, his opponent cheated Kevin by making obvious bad line calls, but Kevin still showed no emotion. His opponent unnecessarily questioned every line call Kevin made, and Kevin made it clear he was unaffected by this. His opponent tried to irritate him by asking him what the score was after every point, when Kevin had clearly verbalized the score. Still, Kevin maintained his poise and focus. In between points, his opponent tried to disrupt Kevin's rhythm by hitting or tossing balls to the far area of the court instead of giving them to him nicely, forcing him to walk further to retrieve them. He also called Kevin names on the changeovers, and yet Kevin was impressively cool as ice. But after all of this expected adversity, his opponent was out of tricks and out of time, and Kevin totally dominated, winning 6–3, 6–2.

It was an extraordinary performance of emotional toughness, which showcased his character and focus. It was inspiring for his teammates and the spectators to see Kevin's superior culture of excellence and his superior disciplined details come together to achieve this incredible display of peak performance.

I was proud to see Kevin transform himself in this match into a leader who became a strong team captain for us in his senior year, following in the footsteps of former captains Skyler Tateishi and Mikey Lim, both of whom Kevin greatly respected. 🎾

CHAPTER 9

KEY NO. 4: STRATEGICAL

"Always start at the end before you begin."
—Robert Kiyosaki

The strategical key deals with how good you are at figuring out the most effective strategies to use that will help you achieve your goals. I have seen many teams work extremely hard but still adopt the wrong plan and fail. Every successful person works hard because hard work works. Working hard is a prerequisite for success.

What's more, leaders and teams who work smart set the foundations for peak performance. But in order to work smart, you consistently need to have the right strategies to achieve your goals. And remember, direction is more important than speed. If you're headed in the right direction and can figure out correct strategies to get where you want to go, you'll achieve your goal eventually.

Work Backwards

One of the big reasons for our 22 consecutive state championship victories is that we had a goal, and I had to work backwards to figure out how to achieve it. Obviously, winning the state championship was our team's overall goal and I would examine all the details that we could control ourselves. For example, there were three distinct parts of our season:

the regular season, the league championship, and the state championship. To have the best chance to win the state championship, our players had to have the best possible seedings. The order they were seeded in the state championship depended on how we finished in our league championship. Getting the best possible results in our league championship depended on our players' seeding in that championship. And those seedings depended on the results we had during the regular season.

Getting the desired results during our regular season depended on our lineup against other schools in order to get head-to-head victories, which directly affected seeding. It wasn't just about randomly writing names on paper and exchanging the lineup with the coach of the opposing team. I would examine all the possibilities of various lineups and the possible effects and outcomes. Everything had to be deliberate and completely calculated. Our success also depended on how well we practiced and prepared every day for these important matches. Moreover, because I would share this with my team, including the concept of working backwards, they knew how critically important every match was and how important every single minute of every day in practice was for us to achieve our goal. They understood that it was about these details, and that every quality practice we did got us one step closer to winning that state championship.

Stay Committed

Sometimes you might have a winning strategy even if you start off losing. If you're running a marathon, the goal is to win the marathon, not the sprint. Some people often win the sprint but lose the marathon. If you're running an actual marathon, depending on your strategy you may be content in fifth place for most of the contest until the final two miles, when you turn up the speed and pass the four frontrunners to win the race. We've all heard the saying, "It's not how you start, but how you finish." (But don't get me wrong—I always prefer a good start *and* a strong finish.)

The point is this: In a football game, your team might have the lead at halftime. You are winning, but you haven't won yet. On the flip side, the other team is losing, but hasn't lost yet. Staying committed to the strategy you believe in for the entire game—if you feel it's working—could very well earn you the victory.

People often say, "If it ain't broke, don't fix it." I've seen a number of businesses and sports teams change a winning strategy unnecessarily, which results in losing or giving up much needed momentum. It's important to understand and be aware of why you are winning or why you are losing. Oftentimes, a player of mine might be losing 3–4 in the first set of a singles match. Well, changing our strategy at that moment might not be the smart thing to do. He's losing the sprint, but everything might be going according to our master plan to win the marathon. Even if he loses the first set, he can still win the next two sets to win the match. It's crucial to stay committed to your strategy if you feel it's the right one, regardless of the score.

Adjust the Sails

If something is clearly not working, it's time to adjust the sails and make a change. If my player loses the first set 1–6, changing our strategy might give us hope in turning things around for the better. Time is also of the essence. During the two-minute coaching break after the first set, I would make a change in strategy to try something different to put my player in a better position to win. In terms of different strategies, we always have a Plan A, B, and C. This is the part of being prepared, and coaching my players to coach themselves. If they can recognize when a strategy change is necessary, maybe they can do so even before talking with me during the coaching breaks. Then we don't waste time using an ineffective strategy and we're able to compete better, increasing our chances of winning.

Speaking of time, sports such as football, basketball, and soccer have time clocks, while sports like volleyball, golf, and tennis don't use them. Because time is an issue in basketball, for example, it definitely affects your strategy depending on who's winning or losing and how much time there is left in the game. A team with a ten-point lead and one minute left in the game might execute a more reliable, less risky strategy to use the clock to their advantage. The losing team might have to be extra aggressive and foul more, because the score and time dictates their strategy to keep that last bit of hope alive.

Volleyball, on the other hand, is different because time is not a factor. In order to come out on top, you need to win a certain number of points in order to win the set in order to win the match. You can be down on match point and still come back and win the match. There's no stalling and running out the clock. You need to win the last point to win the match.

Therefore, sometimes the element of time is often a factor in determining the most effective strategies for you to achieve success. The most successful businesses are thinking long-term. They want to win the marathon. They want to be in business forever, which should be the goal for any company. Just look at how many businesses have closed and gone bankrupt. Remember Blockbuster and RadioShack? What's a big reason for their failure? It's often not recognizing when to adjust the sails and use a different strategy. Having awareness and being able to adapt to different styles and trends in the marketplace allows the best companies to stay on track for long-term success.

One Thing Better

During my junior year at Creighton, we went on a road trip to play against Drake University on their campus in Iowa. Coach Ed put me at number one singles and my opponent was an outstanding player—he was so good that he was also on Canada's Davis Cup team. When I looked across the net, it was obvious to me that he was a much more accomplished player than I was. He had better groundstrokes, volleys, serves, and returns—in addition to being taller and faster.

I thought to myself, *Do I have a chance? How can I win?* On paper, he's definitely going to beat me. Luckily, we don't play a tennis match on paper. We play it in person, face-to-face. So what do I do against him? What kind of strategy can I do to put me in a position to win? Through the years, I learned that I don't have to be better than my opponent at everything. I just have to be better at one thing and keep doing that one thing over and over again. Coach Ed was a master of preparing us for matches and I knew that I was very fit thanks to our many extra hours of conditioning and lifting weights.

So I came up with a strategy to give me hope—to give me that chance to win. I decided that my strategy would be to play a very long match. I wanted to keep him on the court for four hours if I could. You never know what could happen. He could get injured or experience cramping. He could get frustrated and upset with himself. He could get tired and impatient. These were definite possibilities in a long match, but if I lose quickly in a one-hour match, I don't even give these scenarios a chance to materialize. I thought about four-point situations—three that would favor me and one that wouldn't. The three that would be good for me were winning a short point, winning a long point, and losing a long point—the reasoning being that I could play a long point and, if I lost it, still affect his conditioning. The one situation that wouldn't favor me was playing a quick short point that I lost (because I'd lose the point and not affect his conditioning).

Executing this strategy would involve a bit of mathematics. If I directed all of my groundstrokes towards the middle of the court, hitting heavy topspin shots and penetrating slices, I could bisect the angle of his shots so that I could, at least touch the ball. Conversely, if I hit a shot to the corner and I didn't hurt him with it, he would have a greater angle to hit a winner against me, and I probably wouldn't even touch the ball. With this strategy, I could play long points (maybe 20–30 shots per point), which would lead to playing longer games, and a longer match.

On the first point of the match, I executed the strategy perfectly, playing a very long point that involved more than 20 shots. I was committed and continued doing this every single point. I wanted conditioning to become an issue. I was hopeful that my physical toughness would start to affect his mind. We were both playing brilliant tennis in front of a massive crowd of people—who were all cheering for my opponent, by the way. The downside for me was that he won the first set 7–5. The upside was it lasted over an hour and things were going according to plan.

I felt encouraged and was convinced that I knew I had the right strategy to give me a chance to win, even after losing the first set. In the second set, I began to execute my shots even more precisely with more pace and depth down the middle of the court. My goal was to hit shots higher and lower to him, to keep his contact with the ball out of his preferred power zone, just above waist level. Our rallies were grueling and we were both getting winded. I knew that he wanted to beat me badly, especially playing on his home court in front of his fans. But, what he didn't know was that I wanted to beat him even more. The match was now at the two-and-a-half-hour mark and I had set point to even the battle. After another long, tough point, he missed his forehand long and he threw his racket towards the net. I won the second set 7–5 but, more importantly, I witnessed a crack in his armor.

In the third set, I stayed committed to my strategy and was extremely focused mentally during and in between points. He, on the other hand, continued throwing his racket out of frustration and started yelling at himself saying, "This match should have been done two hours ago!" I thought to myself, *Yeah, I got him.* He couldn't take it anymore. He was upset and mad at himself that I was in a position to win. He knew that he was a better athlete and player than me, and it was eating him alive. The battle was just beyond the three-and-a-half-hour mark when I found myself with match point. Needless to say it was another long, tough point and he finally hit his backhand into the net. I won the third set 7–5, walked up to the net to shake hands, and headed quickly for the exit. Looking back, I saw him grab all five rackets out of his bag and slam them into the concrete, cracking every racket. I had a big smile on my face and a satisfying feeling of accomplishment inside.

This is a story that I've shared with countless players over the years to inspire and help them find a way to win. Think about how this applies to business. You don't have to be better than your competitor at everything. You just have to be better at one thing and do that one thing extremely well. The most successful leaders and teams find a way to win even if the odds are against them. So remember, always bet on yourself! ●

CHAPTER 10

KEY NO. 5: TACTICAL

*"Good tactics can save even the worst strategy. Bad
tactics will destroy even the best strategy."*
—George S. Patton

Once you have the right strategy, you need to use
the correct tactics to execute that strategy. Think
of strategy as the general framework needed to
accomplish your goal and tactics as the little
details to help you get there. Some leaders are
good at figuring out the right strategy for their team but still
might suffer a defeat because the right tactics weren't used.
The greatest leaders and teams have disciplined details and
connect the dots completely when determining their strategy
and tactics to achieve victory.

Strengths vs. Weaknesses

In competition, anytime you can use your strengths against
your opponent's weaknesses it will greatly favor you. In tennis
for example, if your opponent's forehand is stronger than their
backhand, a typical strategy might be to play as many shots
to the opponent's backhand as possible. But how do you do
it? Which tactics do you use to allow that scenario to happen
as often as possible? If you just direct every shot towards the
backhand corner, a smart opponent will adjust and ultimately

89

run around the backhand to play more forehand shots from the backhand corner.

So here's the answer. If you're competing against someone equal in ability to you or even better than you, smart shot selections are critical. For example, one tactic might be to play a shot to your opponent's forehand corner. Yes, I know that's their strength. But, once they are in the forehand corner, it completely opens up the backhand corner for your next shot, which will favor you. You might even be able to hit two or more consecutive shots to their backhand before having to again go to their forehand, opening up the backhand side again.

Another tactic might be shot variety—hitting with different spins, depths, heights, and speeds. If your opponent likes playing tennis with a certain rhythm and pace, using shot variety will drive them nuts. Your opponent might like it when you hit the ball really hard over and over again. Their shots might come back to you even harder and faster. Changing your tactic by using shot variety might greatly favor you against an opponent like this.

People exude more confidence in themselves when they know they're good at something. Everyone has certain strengths whether they know it or not. We also have certain weaknesses, which provides an opportunity for improvement to make ourselves better. But let's focus on strengths. The advantage for most successful teams is they're able to use the strengths of their individual team members to collectively help their organization.

For example, if a company's executive team is comprised of ten people, each with one unique strength of expertise, the tactics their CEO employs with them can be vital to the company's success. In order to get peak performance from each team member, the CEO must have a culture where everyone truly enjoys working together, respecting and cherishing each other's strengths. When the executives deeply appreciate each other, it sets up tremendous opportunities to encourage a growth mindset, using various tactics to be more effective and efficient, which leads to peak performance. Looking at things in a different perspective is a good thing. The greatest leaders are always open to different solutions and new possibilities. As the leader, the CEO can facilitate open and constructive discussions to leverage the strengths of individuals to help the team excel. Helping and supporting each other, while empowering the leaders to drive a deeper purpose and meaning in their work, creates an array of tactical options to complement the overall strategy for the team's success.

Adapt to Your Team

Why do some teams with incredibly talented team members lose? And why is it that some teams with only average team talent win? When you have amazing talent on your team and you lose, it's usually because the leader isn't adapting his or her plan to maximize that talent in the best possible way. I've seen many athletic coaches and business leaders fail because they want to stick with their own plan and have their team members adjust instead. However, the best coaches will adapt their plan to consistently highlight the talent of the individual players, to put the team in the best position for success. Knowing the strengths of the people you have and using the best strategical and tactical options to complement your team's talent will always put you in a position to win.

In football, for example, a lower ranked team might defeat a highly rated team and it's viewed as a major upset. What is considered an upset? It's when a team with less talent beats a team with more. That's why sports competitions are held on a field or court instead of played on paper—looking at each team's individual talent and assuming who should win. I've had many occasions when I looked across the net and recognized that my opponent had more talent than me, yet I was able to win with smart play, using effective strategy and tactics.

When I was a kid playing Little League baseball, I noticed how good coaches would put players in the right positions and other coaches would mistakenly put their players in the wrong ones. It doesn't make sense to put an exceptional catcher in right field or a superstar pitcher at second base. Same thing in business. A team member who is an outstanding salesperson should be in a sales position, potentially training and developing other team members to improve their sales techniques. Being able to adapt and use the strengths of your team will consistently put you in favorable positions to achieve success.

Setbacks vs. Comebacks

We've all experienced setbacks at some point in our lives. Whether you've had an injury, a heartbreaking defeat, or an occupational change, it's your mindset that first determines in which direction you're headed. If you have the right mindset and are determined to rise up and recover from the setback, tactics are the little things to keep you moving forward in the right direction. Remember, little things make big differences and big things are often accomplished when you take care of the little things first.

Let me share with you a few setbacks encountered by some notable people. Oprah Winfrey was demoted from her job as a news anchor because the executives said she "wasn't fit for television." Walt Disney was fired from a newspaper for "lacking imagination and having no original ideas." Steve Jobs, at 30 years old, felt devastated and depressed after being unceremoniously removed from the company he started. The Beatles were rejected by Decca Recording Studios who said, "We don't like their sound. They have no future in show business." Michael Jordan, after being cut from his high school basketball team, went home, locked himself in his room, and cried. Henry Ford had two failed car companies prior to succeeding with Ford Motor Company. Albert Einstein wasn't able to speak until he was almost four years old, and his teachers said he would "never amount to much."

During my junior year in college, I tripped over my feet in tennis practice and, as I was falling to the ground, braced my fall with my right hand. It was an instinctual reaction and I knew it was a serious wrist injury (and yes, I am right-handed). After visiting the hospital, the doctor informed me that I had a chipped bone and a torn ligament in my wrist. He put a cast on me that came nearly up to my right shoulder to let the ligament heal. It was a major setback for me. I felt extremely disappointed, as I'd been playing amazing tennis and was enjoying great momentum with my game.

The doctor said I'd be in a cast for two months. (After the first month, I was re-casted with one that came up just below my right elbow.) This was truly depressing for me and affected more than just my tennis game. Writing was a huge challenge, as well as taking a shower and having to wrap my right arm in a plastic bag taped near my shoulder so the cast wouldn't get wet. Sleeping was also an issue, but the worst part was watching my teammates compete and not being able to practice and play with them. Fortunately, I quickly adopted the right mindset to focus on everything else I could do to stay in good physical shape. During tennis practice, I would run, use the stationary bike, and do lots of sit-ups and leg raises to keep my abdominals strong, as well as a ton of plyometric and flexibility exercises.

After two long months, the cast was removed and I immediately began rehab. I was determined to come back stronger than ever and wanted to make sure that the bone chip and ligament had healed properly. I would see the trainers five days a week for my rehab, and I was disciplined to do their suggested additional exercises on my own. After two months and three weeks of no tennis, I finally was able to start hitting tennis balls again and I felt a new appreciation for the game and being healthy. That was the first time I had a major injury that kept me from playing tennis, and I didn't take anything for granted after that. I learned an important lesson: setbacks are opportunities for comebacks.

Chris Ma

In 1995, a year after partnering with senior Taylor Tom and winning the state doubles championship as a freshman, my sophomore singles player Chris Ma went undefeated during the regular season. At the state championship on the Big Island, he continued his streak of winning match after match. After a convincing victory in the semifinals, Chris was ready to face the number one ranked player in the state of Hawai'i in the boys 18 division, a player who was also the defending state singles champion and the tournament's number one seed

Chris Ma

from the Big Island. Chris was ranked number one in the boys 16 division and both players were used to winning.

His opponent had a multitude of weapons in his tennis game. Among his many strengths, he was extremely athletic with a powerful forehand and serve, and played exceptional, aggressive tennis. He really had no weakness. So what would our strategy be? How could I put Chris in a position to win? I told him that this would obviously be a tough challenge, but I knew we could find a way to win. Luckily, Chris looked forward to challenges. He loved it when an opponent played his best tennis, challenging Chris to do the same.

So I shared with him that we needed to do two things as often as possible. First, to direct more shots to his opponent's backhand, because his forehand was very lethal. Second, to be patient in the point by varying the heights of our shots— hitting higher and lower shots with the goal of keeping it out of his power zone, which was a little bit above his waist level. I believe that these two situations would favor Chris in a way where we would win the majority of the points. And of course, if we won the majority of the points, we would win the match. Chris agreed and walked confidently onto the court.

There was a tremendous, lively crowd around the court, eagerly excited to see an intense battle between these two champions. In the first 20 minutes, his opponent destroyed Chris, 6–0. The spectators were shocked at how lopsided this match was. Chris could not even get into position to have a chance to execute our strategy. He couldn't even get into a rally. He'd return his opponent's serve and the shot after that was either a winner or a forced error. When Chris served, his opponent would either hit a return winner or force an error from Chris on that shot or the next. It wasn't pretty. It was actually painful for me to watch because I felt like I was playing the match with Chris. Almost every point finished with a maximum of three or maybe four shots at the most.

After every point Chris lost, I could feel hundreds of eyes watching me to see my reaction. So I stood there cheering him on with a positive expression, though my insides were churning as I imagined what Chris must have felt. I was convinced that we had the right strategy, but we needed to have the right tactics to let him get to the point to execute that strategy.

Immediately after losing the set point, I walked quickly onto the court for the two-minute coaching break. I said, "Chris, I know we have the right strategy but he's just not letting you play. It's all about math and our first two shot selections. We need to bisect the angles of the court and be precise tactically with our first two shots. When you're serving on the deuce and the add side, hit every serve down the middle. Whether he hits his huge forehand or backhand, he's making contact from the middle of the court, which means you'll touch the ball. And if you can touch the ball, you can get into the point to execute our strategy. Also, when you're returning serve, hit every return to the middle of the court for the same reason in bisecting the angles of the court.

"In the first set, you would hit a neutral ball to a corner and he would either hit a powerful forehand from his forehand corner or he'd run around his backhand and hit his favorite inside-out forehand."

I could see that this made perfect sense to Chris, and I walked off the court ready to watch these tactical adjustments in action.

The second set was a completely different story. Chris was executing his shots exactly as we'd discussed. It was amazing to see. Every point became a display of what looked like hard, heavy hitting shots to the average tennis fan, but it really was all about tactics and execution. The spectators could not believe their eyes, as it seemed to be a completely different match than what they'd witnessed in the first set.

"What did you tell Chris?" one of them asked.

Not wanting to share any of our secret details, I simply said, "I told him how to win."

Chris won the second set, 6–3, and I again walked onto the court for the split-set coaching break. I said, "Chris, you're tough and I'm proud of you. Keep doing everything you're doing with your first two shots, but let's add one more thing.

I noticed that when your opponent is going to hit a running backhand, his shot is neutral, which doesn't hurt you and gives us an opportunity to be aggressive. When you see that situation, move forward quickly to play a volley from on or inside the service line. You'll be on offense and you'll definitely win the majority of those points." He agreed, and then it was time to start the third and deciding set.

I overheard some of the spectators saying they couldn't believe how Chris had turned things around. The third set began the way the second one had ended. Chris showed great determination and was executing our tactics and strategy perfectly. Finally, he was up 4–3 with a break point opportunity. Everyone could see that Chris was wearing his opponent down physically, which was leading to mental cracks. I was feeling great watching all of this, but the next thing I saw was Chris lying down on the tennis court. He was in pain with severe leg cramps. I couldn't believe it.

The umpire called an injury time-out and allowed me back onto the court with the trainer. We immediately began massaging Chris's legs to alleviate the pain. Chris needed just five more points to win the match. He only needed to play five more minutes of tennis to win the state singles championship. Once the umpire called time, the trainer and I walked off the court and the boys were ready to continue this epic match.

But the cramps continued and Chris was having great difficulty moving—yet he didn't want to retire the match. He lost the next three games and the third set, 6–4, then hobbled towards the net to congratulate his opponent. Needless to say, it was sad to see such a fantastic match end this way. As I sat down next to Chris, we talked about what had just happened.

"Coach, you were right about the strategy, and the tactical adjustments worked great. I had it. I just needed five more points."

"I know!" I said, knowing we'd been completely prepared for this match. "I don't understand why you cramped. We hydrated properly for a week and it baffles me that you had cramps. Why do you think it happened?"

"Maybe it's because I didn't eat breakfast."

I almost fell out of my chair. "What? Why didn't you eat breakfast?"

"I was feeling kind of nervous and didn't really have an appetite."

"Oh my gosh, Chris! You need to eat to have energy, whether you feel like it or not."

"Well, Coach, at least we clinched the state team championship yesterday." This kind of selfless thinking typified why Chris was such an amazing team player for our team. He went on to win the state singles championship the following year as a junior, and as a senior won the state doubles championship. In fact, that state singles championship match that he cramped up in as a sophomore was his only loss during his entire varsity tennis career. 🎾

◆

CHAPTER 11

KEY NO. 6: ENVIRONMENTAL

*"When a flower doesn't bloom you fix the environment
in which it grows, not the flower."*
—Alexander Den Heijer

The environmental key means creating the right atmosphere for your team, even as you deal with outside forces beyond your control. As head coach, I wanted to create a safe and friendly environment for my players and their families, as well as the other students and their families, so they always looked forward to coming to our tennis facility. It was so gratifying to consistently see so many students and parents socializing with one another in such a positive, welcoming environment. This is such an important part of peak performance. Even if you have the other five keys, if your team doesn't feel right about their environment, and if they can't properly deal with forces beyond their control, they won't perform up to their full potential.

It's Your People

In order to have the right team environment, everyone needs to play a role. To help the team achieve its goals, every individual needs to contribute in making an impact. Everyone wants to be a part of something special and significant. That's why people love participating on a team. But that's only if the team leader is fair and truly cares about the well-being of each individual. As the leader, it's your responsibility to create a healthy, safe, and positive atmosphere, because they're *your* people. It's just as you'd do with your family at home—your team is your second family away from home.

Creating an environment that fosters collaboration and cohesion allows your team the opportunity to accomplish anything they set their minds to. Moreover, encouraging them to contribute innovative, creative ideas—thereby helping the team find different and better ways to achieve goals—deepens the commitment of each team member. My 12 players, assistant coach, and every player's parent had roles on our team, which built strong team support for everyone involved.

In creating your environment, it's extremely vital to acknowledge the behaviors you value. At Punahou School's annual athletic awards assembly, each coach would present one team member with the Most Inspirational Player award, as voted upon by his or her teammates. And local businesses might have their own annual or semiannual awards, acknowledging team members who demonstrated special resiliency, team-work, creativity, perseverance, integrity, compassion, humility, and courage. At Punahou's tennis complex, the sportsmanship trophies on display were significantly bigger in size than the championship trophies. In these and other ways, leaders can create a positive environment and highlight the accomplish-ments of their team members, fostering the atmosphere that they want to create and, more importantly, sustain.

In the University of Oregon's sports complex, Hawai'i football star Marcus Mariota's Heisman Trophy is on display. What's fascinating is the inverted pyramid at the base of the trophy. At the bottom of this pyramid, near the point, is the name Mariota. Stacked above that are various layers of recognition: names of Little League baseball teams Mariota played with, names of numerous coaches who helped him, and names of teachers and other mentors who believed in him. At the very top level are the names of every teammate from the 2014 Oregon Ducks football team. Every player on offense,

KEY NO. 6: ENVIRONMENTAL

defense, and special teams is listed on the base of Mariota's Heisman Trophy.

If you view this incredible display from above, you'll also see a rendering of his home state. Mariota has noted that all of Hawai'i's people played a key role in his success in winning the prestigious Heisman. Those people helped and encouraged him to believe in himself, which made him the person he is today. This amazing display showcases how important coaches and a positive team environment can be in helping someone excel and reach his or her full potential. Best of all, it can be contagious, sending the right message to others who want to strive for excellence.

Expect the Unexpected

I liked seeing my players practice in the toughest conditions. Practicing on an extra hot day with high humidity or in very windy conditions made my players tougher and better in dealing with such challenging situations, should they be a factor on match day. On a very windy day, for example, I'd often tell my team, "We might not be able to play our best tennis on a day like this, but neither will our opponents. To gain the advantage, we just need to deal with the wind a little bit better than they do to get the upper hand. Even though we might not feel or play at our peak, we can always give it our best." Heat, cold, wind, humidity, light drizzle, and snow flurries are literally environmental conditions that many athletes experience during competition and I would frequently remind my team that the best excuse is the one you never make.

But what about in the business world? Can you deal with the pressure of deadlines, shifting market conditions, and other unforeseen circumstances that can and will arise when you least expect it? If you always expect things to go smoothly and according to plan, you will consistently be disappointed. The key is to expect the unexpected. If you have the mindset that you expect adversity and challenges on a daily basis, you'll be able to deal with them in a much more favorable way. Problems are inevitable. You must condition yourself and your team to be problem solvers.

Think about the environment you're in right now. Is it very hectic and chaotic? Do you constantly feel stress and pressure? Do you get sidetracked because things arise that need your attention, which causes you to alter your plan for the day? If your response to these questions is yes, then you were probably expecting your day to go according to plan. But whether you're in sports or business, things rarely do. You must be able to adapt and adjust if you want to be productive and succeed. The best leaders and teams are prepared for everything and anything that could happen and know how they will respond. They're expecting it. They understand their internal and external environments and can properly deal with the unexpected. They become comfortable in what others perceive as uncomfortable situations.

Look Within Yourself

During my senior year at Creighton, we traveled to Lake of the Ozarks to play the University of Missouri. It was a gorgeous sunny spring day at a beautiful country club. We usually played six singles matches first, followed by three doubles matches next, with the best of nine winning the day. However, another dual match before ours was running overtime, and because there were three courts available right then, the coaches decided to play the three doubles matches first.

My partner, Rick Faust, and I played great together and won in straight sets. Our team had a 2–1 lead after the doubles matches, and we were feeling hopeful going into singles. Coach Ed had me at number one singles against Missouri's number one, who boasted a high national college ranking. Time was ticking away in my college tennis career and I had only a few more months before I graduated, so I wanted to savor each and every match I played. Playing college tennis, traveling to different parts of the country, was one of the best experiences of my life. Needless to say, I was fired up and ready to give it my best against Missouri's best.

My opponent was a super strong, talented player who appeared to have no weaknesses. In fact, he and I had the same style of play, and winning would depend on who executed better. I honestly felt that he was a notch better than me, although I was playing the best tennis of my entire college career. I had poise and confidence in myself and as the match began, I rose to the occasion. I was matching him shot for shot, and if I could sustain that, I believed I had a chance to win. In all honesty, if we played each other ten times, I felt that he'd probably beat me nine times out of ten. But I didn't have to play him ten times. I didn't need to beat him ten times. I just needed to beat him one time—today!

The first set was an incredible display of power, control, finesse, and fight. We both were executing heavy, aggressive groundstrokes and taking advantage of shorter balls and putting those shots away with piercing volleys and punishing overheads at the net. After an hour and 15 minutes, he used one of those volleys to close out the first set 7–5. The first set was so close I felt it could easily have gone my way, had I executed two or three shots better.

The second set was much like the first. In fact, we were both exhibiting the first five keys of peak performance brilliantly. Physically, he and I were showcasing our entire arsenal of shots, grinding out every single point, and using good footwork to continue hitting these precise shots with power and finesse. Mentally, we seemed about equal—our concentration and focus on the task at hand was like a mirror image. Emotionally, we were both controlling our internal climate and getting pumped up, using it to fuel us at the right moments. Strategically, we both seemed to have an identical plan. It would just come down to which of us would carry it out better. Obviously, he felt that he could play his game to beat me, and I felt I could play mine to beat him. Tactically, we were trying to do the same things to each other; it would all depend on the execution. And on that score, I connected on some important points and won the second set 7–5.

Just before the third set, I looked over to the side of the court and saw my entire team sitting there next to the Missouri team. It dawned on me that the rest of my teammates had completed their matches and that mine was the last one to finish. We had already passed the two-and-a-half-hour mark and the crowd was getting loud and rowdy. My teammates were looking at me, yelling, "Let's go, O Captain! My Captain!" (That was an Ethan Hawke line from the *Dead Poets Society*, and that's what the other players called me as team captain.) The Missouri team was yelling encouragement to my opponent, as were most of the other spectators. That's the moment my opponent and I realized the team match score was tied 4-4, and we were the deciding match.

This is when the sixth key about environment became very evident. The only spectators cheering for me were my coaches and teammates, a total of nine people. The other 200-plus onlookers were cheering for my opponent. In fact, it no longer felt like a tennis match, with the usual etiquette. It felt more like a football game, with some extremely vocal fans. That's just how it was, and I had to deal with it.

In the first game of the third set, I ran wide to hit a backhand, rolled my left ankle, and fell to the ground. I tried to walk it off but I immediately knew that this was a bad injury. I mean it was really bad! I could barely put any weight on my left foot. Looking over to my teammates, I could see their faces in shock and their hopes of a huge team victory evaporated. I felt completely deflated and majorly disappointed but I wasn't about to retire the match. It didn't even cross my mind, even though I couldn't step into my forehands, push off my back foot to hit backhands, or spring up on my serve. Dejected, I began to think, *I can't, I can't, I can't!* and I quickly fell behind, 0–4.

Then, as I was preparing for the next game, I looked over and saw how defeated my teammates looked. I felt helpless and defeated as well, like I was letting them down as their captain and teammate. I was two games away from losing the match, but more painfully, our team match. A victory would have been the biggest win in our team's history, for sure.

As I was toweling off by the back fence, Coach Ed walked over and said, "Instead of worrying about the things you can't do, focus on what you still *can* do!" Then he walked away. He said this in a very powerful and forceful voice, the only words he spoke to me during the entire match. I digested what he'd said and thought, *That's brilliant! If I can't step in on my forehands, I can put all of my weight on my right foot and hit open stance forehands. If I can't push off my back foot on my backhands, I can put all the weight on my right foot and hit open stance backhands. If I can't spring up on my serve, I can put all the weight on my right foot and make a lower contact to serve.*

I figured out these adjustments and they all made perfect sense. But was it too late? Up to this point in the third set, my opponent had made me run extra because of my injury and limited court coverage. It actually took him out of his game plan, because he figured the injury meant he was on his way to victory. But after Coach Ed's words of wisdom, I won the next game. After winning that one, I thought, *At least I won't lose this set 6–0.* Then I won another game and was down 2–4, and on the next changeover I was only down 3–4. Now the environment was getting really crazy. Everyone in the crowd was screaming, banging seats, just making noise. It was intense and even though I'd won those three games, I was still two games away from losing.

Maybe it was the adrenaline, but now I was also executing my shots better after making those adjustments. My opponent was definitely feeling the pressure, because I was coming back! With all the drama, this match was going to be epic even if I ended up losing. It was at this moment I realized I wanted to beat not just my opponent, but all of the 200-plus people cheering against me. And the only way to do it was to continue to fight for every single shot in every single point. I wanted to win this match for Coach Ed and my teammates and make it the most monumental college match that these spectators had ever seen.

After winning the next two games, I was ahead 5–4. As I sat on the bench drinking water on the changeover, I looked across the court at my teammates. I was using them as inspiration, reflecting back on all the hard work, sweat, and pain we'd experienced together to get to this moment. From that point on, there was no denying me. After winning match point, I felt overwhelmed as I shook hands and hugged my opponent at the net. I had earned his respect, along with that of all his supporters, and they congratulated me as I left the court. They told me that I'd shown heart, determination, resiliency, and toughness. They told me they were inspired by my comeback, especially in that boisterous pro-Missouri environment.

The next day, I was on the front page in the sports section of the *Omaha World-Herald*. Coach Ed had a quote in there: "It was a good learning experience for our younger players. They were all there sitting and watching the whole thing. He was beaten. It was a really good comeback." Coach Ed's advice to me that day is something that I'll never forget. I've used it countless times with my players to inspire them to always focus on what they can do, not what they can't. 🎾

CHAPTER 12

INSPIRING HOPE

"Only in the darkness can you see the stars."
—Martin Luther King Jr.

D o you know the most valuable four-letter word in all our lives? It's "hope"—something we all need plenty of. One of the most important things a great coach does is inspire hope in his or her team. If your team thinks they have a chance to win, then success becomes a possibility. If your team thinks they have no chance, then your team has lost even before the game begins. Hope is a powerful thing, encouraging you to navigate your path to victory. There's always a way to win. It's your job as the coach to show it to them. Give them a clear vision of the mission. Show them the light at the end of the tunnel. And remind them that when the odds are against you, never bet on the odds. Always bet on yourself!

Seeing the Light

All of us experience adversity and challenges in our lives and some people experience deeper levels than others. Hitting rock bottom in your life may or may not happen to you, but if it did, how would you deal with it? What if the unimaginable occurred? Could you rise up and keep a positive perspective? What if you had not one but two major accidents that would change your life forever? You might know someone who lived through something inconceivable and you observed how they responded, either in a good way or a bad one.

W Mitchell is someone who truly inspires me and I know will inspire you as well. W was a good-looking young man, and on July 19, 1971, something happened in San Francisco that would change his life forever. He was riding his newly purchased motorcycle at 65 miles an hour when he was distracted for a split second and crashed into a laundry truck that had turned in front of him. He suffered only minor injuries, but then the motorcycle's gas cap popped off and W Mitchell was turned into a human fireball. Two-thirds of his skin burned off. He lost most of his fingers and thumbs because they were burned to the knuckles, and his face was completely disfigured.

I would have to say that most people in his condition would have given up in life, but not W Mitchell. He was determined to focus on the good in his life and made a decision to start his own business. Within three years, he became a millionaire. He also learned how to fly airplanes and completed his first solo aircraft flight. Then one clear, chilly Colorado morning, November 11, 1975, he took three passengers on a flight, not realizing there was a thin layer of ice on the wings. The plane crashed soon after takeoff and three people walked away. He wasn't one of them. He had injured his spinal cord, leaving him paralyzed from the waist down, with zero hope for recovery. Because he no longer needed his toes, the doctors cut them off and sewed them onto his hands. In addition, his wife left him, commenting that she couldn't be with a "fried cripple." After all of this, W Mitchell still refused to give up and was subsequently elected mayor of Crested Butte, Colorado. Soon after, he found the woman of his dreams and made her his wife.

Because of his experiences, W Mitchell has been a compelling motivational speaker for many years, inspiring hope in countless others who have their own challenges and difficulties to overcome in life. He famously said, "Before I was paralyzed, there were 10,000 things I could do. Now there are 9,000. I can either dwell on the 1,000 I've lost or focus on the 9,000 I have left." He also said, "It's not what happens to you, it's what you do about it." His story always reminds me to see the light in the darkest of situations. How many times can you get knocked down and keep choosing to get up? Life is definitely not easy and often not fair, but life is life and each of us has the choice to take control of our life and live.

Life Happens For You

When bad things occur in life, most people blame that situation for happening and feel sorry for themselves. But if you view life in that perspective, you can't truly welcome adversities and life's challenges correctly. Life doesn't happen *to* you. Life happens *for* you. W Mitchell had two major adversities in his life and because of those "unfortunate" accidents, he found his true purpose in life by inspiring millions of people to bounce back from every tragic situation or setback they might experience. Some people have the victim mindset and think, *It's not fair. I can never win. Why did this happen to me?* Remember, life happens. It's how we respond that matters. That's the difference between winning and losing in the biggest, most important game of all—life. Are you winning or losing in your game of life?

In order to win in the game of life, you need to change from a *victim* mindset into a *victor* mindset. We can't control things in life that are beyond our control. A devastating hurricane, flood, or fire might cause you to lose your house and all of your irreplaceable possessions. You might be involved in a serious car accident, resulting in a long rehabilitation process. You might receive word from your doctor that you have a cancerous tumor. You might be laid off because of financial cutbacks at your company. The normal response from most people in these situations is the victim mindset. But this is when you start to lose in the game of life. You need to flip it into the victor mindset by finding the good in what most would perceive as a bad situation. When you can live your life thinking that life happens for you, this attitude becomes contagious for everyone close to you and you'll inspire others to be victors in their own lives.

It reminds me of a quote from the great Bruce Lee, who said, "When you find yourself in a room surrounded by your enemies you should tell yourself, 'I am not locked in here with you, you are locked in here with me.'" This is the kind of mindset you should have if you want to succeed in life. Get rid of that victim mentality.

I also like to look at that quote in a slightly different perspective, by changing "your enemies" to "unfortunate situations." Whether you are dealing with unfortunate situations in your life or helping someone deal with theirs, the victor mindset is paramount. We can inspire hope in others if we have built trust with them. If they believe in us, we can believe in them and help them believe in themselves. Belief is extremely powerful, but so is doubt. Choose to be around people with positive energy who consistently lift you up to see the possibilities, instead of negative people who bring you down and make you feel hopeless. Inspiring others to motivate themselves to see the positives in their lives, feeling valued and living with dignity, is very impactful. By reinforcing the victor mindset, you can make a priceless difference in others because they trust you and know that you have empathy for them.

Building Relationships

When someone's on his deathbed, what's the most important thing to him at that moment? Is it money? Is it his fancy cars? Is it his big, expensive house? It doesn't seem to be any of these but, instead, it's the relationships they've built with other people over the years. He wants to see his family and true friends. He wants to see people he loves and cares about. Now, if that's the most important thing at the end of our lives, shouldn't we prioritize the importance of building meaningful relationships *during* our lives?

Think about the people in your life right now. If you

desperately need someone's help, who would you call? Who would be there for you without a doubt? Those are the people with whom you have built the deepest, most meaningful relationships. Those are the ones you can depend on, and they know you'd be there for them too. I absolutely know the people in my life I can depend on if I need help.

Because of the importance of building relationships, I want to inspire and help as many people as I can in the world to live better, healthier, more meaningful lives. I want to inspire hope in everyone so that, in turn, they can inspire hope in others. People who feel hopeless also feel helpless. But it's often a mindset that can help someone who's living in darkness into seeing the light. It's the relationship of showing that you care and taking time to encourage others to see that one positive among 20 negatives. It's inspiring them to focus on ways to get through their adversity. Life naturally has ups and downs for all of us, but we need to focus on the ups, not the downs. Tough times never last, but tough people do. Many people see clouds and storms, but champions always see the sun peeking through. These champions have learned to dance in the rain, and I want to challenge you to do the same. Always look at it as an opportunity to turn what might appear hopeless into hope.

Also, think about this. If today were the last day of your life, would you still want to do what you're about to do today? And, whom would you want to be doing it with? These are deep, meaningful questions that you need to periodically ask yourself to make sure you're living the life you want. You might be making others happy, but are you making yourself happy? I've seen some people live miserable lives, often disappointed because they're waiting for someone else to make them happy. Rather than waiting for someone to give you flowers, plant your own garden. Instead of relying on others to make you happy and do something nice for you, focus on making yourself happy. I mean truly happy. When you can assure true happiness for yourself, you will have even better relationships with others. And, happy people live longer, are healthier, and are more productive. ✿

CHAPTER 13

REMOVING THE LINES

"The impossible is what nobody can do
until somebody does it."
—Anonymous

A football field and a tennis court have lines and boundaries. A business has parameters. I want everyone to focus on going beyond the lines, beyond the parameters to affect what happens inside the lines, inside the parameters. That's how you can improve the productivity and performance of your team. That's how you affect results, which leads to winning. That's how you can have peak performance to achieve and sustain success. That's how you can find greatness.

But, what if we remove the lines? What if we allow ourselves to think that there are no parameters? That there are no boundaries and anything can be achieved and everything we can imagine could become reality. That's how things get invented. That's how records get broken. This type of thinking is how things that seem to be impossible become possible. The greatest leaders are visionaries. They think outside the box, or as I say, beyond the lines. So whatever you are currently doing, imagine removing the lines and visualize what the possibilities could really be.

Character and Courage

Character is who you are. It is of utmost importance in everything you do. People and teams with great character also have great respect from others. The most important traits involve moral character—honor, integrity, fidelity, honesty, loyalty, humility, compassion, caring, respect for others, and trustworthiness. It's simple. You either have great moral character or you don't. This is the essence of remarkable people, and these traits can never be compromised.

Having courage is imperative. There's never a wrong time to do the right thing and you need to do the right thing all the time. I always told my teams that we could do 99 things right but, if we did one wrong thing, everyone would remember only that one. So we simply don't do it. When you have courage to make difficult decisions, you probably won't make everyone happy, but everyone will respect you and the decision you've made. For example, if the president of Punahou School had a son trying out for my varsity tennis team, who didn't earn his spot after going through the tryout process, he wouldn't make the team. Fair is fair. There's no favoritism, because everyone is equal. Everyone had the same fair tryout to make the team, regardless of who their parents are. That speaks loud and clear about the character of a leader, and having courage to do what's right. Can you always do the right thing with your team so they don't lose the respect they have for you? Once respect is lost, it's usually gone forever.

At Wimbledon in London, above the player's entrance to the prestigious Centre Court, there are two lines from Rudyard Kipling's poem "If": *If you can meet with triumph and disaster and treat those two imposters just the same.* Here is this wonderful poem in its entirety.

> If you can keep your head when all about you
> Are losing theirs and blaming it on you,
> If you can trust yourself when all men doubt you,
> But make allowance for their doubting too;

113

If you can wait and not be tired by waiting,
Or being lied about, don't deal in lies,
Or being hated, don't give way to hating,
And yet don't look too good, nor talk too wise:

If you can dream—and not make dreams your master;
If you can think—and not make thoughts your aim;
If you can meet with Triumph and Disaster
And treat those two imposters just the same;
If you can bear to hear the truth you've spoken
Twisted by knaves to make a trap for fools,
Or watch the things you gave your life to, broken,
And stoop and build 'em up with worn-out tools:

If you can make one heap of all your winnings
And risk it on one turn of pitch-and-toss,
And lose, and start again at your beginnings
And never breathe a word about your loss;
If you can force your heart and nerve and sinew
To serve your turn long after they are gone,
And so hold on when there is nothing in you
Except the Will which says to them: "Hold on!"

If you can talk with crowds and keep your virtue,
Or walk with Kings—nor lose the common touch,
If neither foes nor loving friends can hurt you,
If all men count with you, but none too much;
If you can fill the unforgiving minute
With sixty seconds' worth of distance run,
Yours is the Earth and everything that's in it,
And—which is more—you'll be a Man, my son!

I truly love the depth and meaning of this poem (and not just because two of its lines are inscribed at Wimbledon). Life definitely has its ups and downs, but what's important is living a balanced, honorable life. Being able to look at yourself in the mirror and truly know that you are the best person you can be—that you are courageous and exhibit the highest values and principles—will give you peace of mind, let you live your brand, and let you inspire others as a role model.

My 1% Principle

How do good teams become great? How does someone who is great become extraordinary? It happens when you push beyond your limits. You are capable of doing more than you think. My 1% Principle is simple to understand and leads to extraordinary results. Can you give 1% more effort today than you did yesterday? Can you accomplish 1% more than last week? Can you improve 1% on a current weakness? Can you add 1% more knowledge by learning something new today? It's as simple as running one lap on the track. The next time you're on the track, run one lap plus a quarter lap. The next time run one lap and a half. Next time, run one lap plus three-quarters. Soon you'll be running one mile. Before you know it, running five miles will be routine and perhaps even running a marathon might become a possibility. But how did it all start? It started with the 1% Principle.

What if you're in the gym lifting weights? You might begin doing two sets of ten repetitions of bicep curls at a comfortable weight. One week later, you might increase the weight, or keep the same weight and add more repetitions. A week after that, you keep pushing your limits smartly and you are well on your way to improving your strength.

Bruce Lee and one of his students would run three miles every day. One day, they were close to hitting their usual three-mile mark when Bruce said, "Let's do two more." Extremely fatigued, his student responded, "I'll die if I run two more." Bruce's response to his student was, "Then do it." After running the two extra miles, his student was completely exhausted and a bit angry because of Bruce's comment. "Quit and you might as well be dead," Bruce explained. "If you always put limits on what you can do, physical or anything else, it'll spread over into the rest of your life. It'll spread into your work, into your morality, into your entire being. There are no limits. There are plateaus, but you must not stay there; you must go beyond them. If it kills you, it kills you. A man must constantly exceed his level."

The point is this: Whatever you do, you can always do more. But, do it in a smart way. If you haven't run for two years, don't do a ten-mile run. If you haven't been in the gym for a while, don't overdo it. That's how careless injuries happen. You might have the right intent for improvement but it's not about doing big things immediately. It's doing the little things that lead you towards achieving the big things. Here's an example of a little thing. At sea level, water is extremely hot at 211 degrees, but at 212 degrees, it boils. When it boils, you also have steam. When you have steam, you can power a locomotive. That's the big difference that one extra degree makes.

As a leader, I would consistently focus on using my 1% Principle to improve my team and myself. I always keep in mind the quote, "Do not follow where the path may lead. Go instead where there is no path and leave a trail." We can learn from other successful people and championship teams, but making yourself and your team unique to outdo what others have done puts you in a position to accomplish extraordinary things. The big positive effect for everyone is that it causes a higher tide where all boats rise. Successful people and teams will learn and examine possibilities they never thought could be accomplished. This is critically important because there are still many things in life that haven't been discovered, invented, or achieved. Pushing your limits in everything you do and imagining the possibilities of what could be, you must erase the lines of what has already been proven and accomplished.

I strongly believe that sometimes the smallest step in the right direction becomes the biggest step of your life. I have seen this with many people as well as in my own life—a 1% step in the right direction can set us on a trajectory for unprecedented achievement and success. By improving yourself and committing to the 1% Principle, you become more open and exposed to different and new possibilities, and therefore better outcomes in your life.

Explore the Possibilities

A man decided he was going to climb to the top of a very tall tree. He had never climbed a tree before and a crowd of people had gathered, shouting at him, "It's impossible! You'll never be able to do it!" But the man persevered, climbed the tree, and reached the top. How did he do it? He was deaf and thought that everybody was simply encouraging him to reach his goal.

If we want to achieve something we've never achieved before, we need to try things we've never tried before. The greatest people become even greater because they are always open to creative ideas, different solutions, and exploring new possibilities. It doesn't matter what other people say (and sometimes they might say you're crazy) but it depends on you and what you believe you can do.

Apple's Steve Jobs said, "Everything around you that you call life was made up by people that were no smarter than you. And you can change it. You can influence it. You can build your own things that other people can use. And the minute that you understand that you can poke life—if you push in and something will pop out on the other side—that you can change it and you can mold it. That maybe the most important thing is to shake off this erroneous notion that life is there and you're just going to live in it versus embrace it, change it, improve it, and make your mark upon it. I think that's very important and once you learn it, you will want to change life and make it better."

Elon Musk is the CEO of Tesla and founder of SpaceX, who is going above and beyond by using his imagination about what can possibly be achieved, then turning it into reality. Musk is definitely poking life and seeing what pops out the other side. He has revolutionized electric cars and is making tremendous progress in designing and refining rockets and spacecraft, with the ultimate goal of enabling people to live on other planets. He is our present-day Albert Einstein, exploring heretofore unimaginable possibilities and turning his dreams into our reality.

Find Your Greatness

I love greatness. I love helping people on their quests to reach greatness. So how does someone achieve greatness? You can't build the tallest, most beautiful skyscraper on a small foundation. You need a big foundation in order to build the best skyscraper in the world. And there's tremendous competition to see who can literally build the tallest, greatest, most unique skyscraper. But finding your own greatness isn't about competing against someone else. It's internal. It's your feeling fulfilled. It's finding your purpose in life and making an impact in helping others be better. It's making a positive difference in the world.

Some people do great things, but all of us can do little things in a great way. And sometimes, average, ordinary people can inspire a movement, which will impact the world in an invaluable way. For example, when you're walking down the street and come across a piece of trash, do you pick it up or walk past it? If you pick up three pieces of trash every day, will it make a big impact in keeping your community cleaner? Can one person really make a difference? If you did this simple thing daily, you will have picked up 1,095 pieces of trash every year. If one thousand people did this, they'd pick up 1,095,000 pieces of trash. If you inspired one million people to do this, there would be 1,095,000,000 fewer pieces of trash in our world every year. So yes, average people can make a significant difference in society.

During our tennis season, my players and I volunteered at the Special Olympics on the University of Hawai'i campus.

Watching these athletes give their best effort in competition is truly inspiring to see. Even more inspiring is their support and encouragement for each other. They really have no limits. If they believe they can do it, they can. I like having my players watch these Special Olympic athletes, because they are witnessing greatness in motion and because it helps keep them focused on the big picture in life. Whatever you do, give it your best and enjoy doing it. With the Special Olympics athletes, it's clear that the limits they have only exist in their own minds. If you haven't been to a Special Olympics event, I highly encourage you to go—and take your team with you.

Greatness is exemplified in a variety of ways and comes in all sizes and forms. My mom is an example—I know she loves me and would do anything for me. I greatly admire my sister Lori, a single mother, for raising her daughter Naia in the best possible way, showing her love and, like our mom, doing anything for her. People often show their greatness for another person by donating a kidney, volunteering for a bone marrow transplant, or giving blood. Other people show their greatness by purchasing food for the homeless or donating their time working at a charity. Whatever the case, it comes down to doing something special for the benefit of someone who needs help.

I remember hearing a story about a blind girl who hated herself and her life. The only person she didn't hate was her boyfriend, because he loved her and was always there to help her. One day, she told him that if she could somehow see the world, she would love to marry him. When she received an anonymous donation of a pair of eyes a few weeks later, she was of course absolutely ecstatic, now able to see everything and everyone in the world around her. Seeing her boyfriend for the first time, she was completely stunned to see that *he* was blind. "Now that you can see the world," he said, "will you marry me?" But to his great surprise, she didn't accept his proposal. He walked off, crushed and heartbroken. A few days later, she received a letter from him in the mail: "Please take good care of my eyes, dear."

Finding greatness is something we must first find in ourselves. Jennifer Lopez is a famous singer, dancer, actress, producer, and businesswoman, someone who has definitely found her greatness. "If I told you all the people who told me I wasn't going to act or sing or dance or I wasn't good at it or that I should stop or I should quit," she told an interviewer, "even after I became famous for doing these things! The truth is nobody knows what's inside of you. Only you know what's inside of you. Only you know what you can accomplish and what you're capable of and what your gut and your dreams and your desires and your wants and your ability. You only know. Nobody else knows. So whatever you feel in your heart and in your gut, you should follow that. Then, if that changes one day, that's fine too. Then you follow that. Everything I did there was no box for and there was no map for and that was a good thing. You don't need so much to do something anybody's done before. You can blaze your own path."

We have a unique superpower within all of us—our greatness. We need to search for it and once we find it, we'll be able to empower ourselves in helping countless others. By going beyond the game, we can achieve and sustain peak performance in everything we do and, by removing the lines, we can surely explore the true potential in ourselves and our teams. When you build a solid foundation of strong values, principles, and disciplines, you give yourself the opportunity to achieve anything and everything you set your mind to. You, as a leader, currently view yourself as average, good, or great. But I guarantee that all of us can be better.

So here's my challenge to you. I want you to closely examine your life right now to see how you can strive for the highest level of excellence in finding your greatness, and once you do, help others find theirs. 🏀